D0535851

J
92
MUIR

Ito, Tom.

The importance of John Muir.

cl

Desert Foothills Library
P.O. Box 4070
Cave Creek, AZ 85331
488-2286

THE IMPORTANCE OF

John Muir

These and other titles are included in The Importance
Of biography series:

THE IMPORTANCE OF

John Muir

by
Tom Ito

Desert Foothills Library
P.O. Box 4070
Cave Creek, AZ 85331

Lucent Books, P.O. Box 289011, San Diego, CA 92198-9011

Library of Congress Cataloging-in-Publication Data

Ito, Tom.
　　John Muir　/　by Tom Ito.
　　　　p.　cm. — (The Importance of)
　　Includes bibliographical references and index.
　　ISBN 1-56006-054-9
　　1. Muir, John, 1838-1914—Juvenile literature.
　2. Conservationists—United States—Biography—Juvenile
literature.　3. Naturalists—United States—Biography—
Juvenile literature.　[1. Muir, John, 1838-1914.
2. Naturalists.　3. Conservationists.]　I. Title.　II. Series.
QH31.M78I86　　1996
333.7'2'092—dc20
　　[B]　　　　　　　　　　　　　　　　　　94-23489
　　　　　　　　　　　　　　　　　　　　　　CIP
　　　　　　　　　　　　　　　　　　　　　　AC

Copyright 1996 by Lucent Books, Inc., P.O. Box 289011,
San Diego, California, 92198-9011

Printed in the U.S.A.

No part of this book may be reproduced or used in any other
form or by any other means, electrical, mechanical, or otherwise, including, but not limited to, photocopy, recording, or
any information storage and retrieval system, without prior
written permission from the publisher.

Contents

Foreword

THE IMPORTANCE OF biography series deals with individuals who have made a unique contribution to history. The editors of the series have deliberately chosen to cast a wide net and include people from all fields of endeavor. Individuals from politics, music, art, literature, philosophy, science, sports, and religion are all represented. In addition, the editors did not restrict the series to individuals whose accomplishments have helped change the course of history. Of necessity, this criterion would have eliminated many whose contribution was great, though limited. Charles Darwin, for example, was responsible for radically altering the scientific view of the natural history of the world. His achievements continue to impact the study of science today. Others, such as Chief Joseph of the Nez Percé, played a pivotal role in the history of their own people. While Joseph's influence does not extend much beyond the Nez Percé, his nonviolent resistance to white expansion and his continuing role in protecting his tribe and his homeland remain an inspiration to all.

These biographies are more than factual chronicles. Each volume attempts to emphasize an individual's contributions both in his or her own time and for posterity. For example, the voyages of Christopher Columbus opened the way to European colonization of the New World. Unquestionably, his encounter with the New World brought monumental changes to both Europe and the Americas in his day. Today, however, the broader impact of Columbus's voyages is being critically scrutinized. *Christopher Columbus,* as well as every biography in The Importance Of series, includes and evaluates the most recent scholarship available on each subject.

Each author includes a wide variety of primary and secondary source quotations to document and substantiate his or her work. All quotes are footnoted to show readers exactly how and where biographers derive their information, as well as provide stepping stones to further research. These quotations enliven the text by giving readers eyewitness views of the life and times of each individual covered in The Importance Of series.

Finally, each volume is enhanced by photographs, bibliographies, chronologies, and comprehensive indexes. For both the casual reader and the student engaged in research, The Importance Of biographies will be a fascinating adventure into the lives of people who have helped shape humanity's past and present, and who will continue to shape its future.

IMPORTANT DATES IN THE LIFE OF JOHN MUIR

1838
John Muir is born in Dunbar, Scotland, April 21.

1849
Emigrates with his family to the United States and settles in Wisconsin.

1860
Wins prize for inventions at the Wisconsin State Agricultural Fair; enters University of Wisconsin.

1867
Walks from Kentucky to Florida and writes first journal.

1868
Arrives in San Francisco, California, March 28.

1869–1873
Decides to make Yosemite Valley his headquarters and explores the Sierra Nevada for evidence of glacial activity.

1874–1878
Climbs Mount Shasta; launches movement for federal control of forests.

1879
Embarks on first trip to Alaska.

1880
Marries Louise Wanda Strentzel; makes second trip to Alaska.

1881
Explores Arctic waters; first daughter, Annie Wanda, is born.

1882–1887
Operates family ranch; success in fruit tree cultivation.

1886
Second daughter, Helen, is born.

1888
Ascends Mount Rainier.

1889
Works for the creation of Yosemite National Park.

1890
Yosemite National Park established by Congress; explores Muir Glacier in Alaska.

1891–1892
Founds Sierra Club; works for recession of Yosemite Valley.

1893–1894
Publishes *The Mountains of California*.

1899
Joins Harriman expedition to Alaska.

1901
Publishes *Our National Parks*.

1903–1904
Guides President Roosevelt through Yosemite; begins fight to save Hetch Hetchy Valley and makes world tour.

1905
Recession of Yosemite Valley to federal government; Louie Muir dies.

1909
Short story "Stickeen" is published.

1911
Publishes *My First Summer in the Sierra*.

1912
Publishes *The Yosemite*.

1913
Publishes *The Story of My Boyhood and Youth*; loses fight to save Hetch Hetchy Valley.

1914
Dies in Los Angeles on December 24.

Devoted to Preserving the Purity of Nature

John Muir, naturalist and activist, came to the United States as a young immigrant from Scotland in the early nineteenth century and devoted the rest of his long life to the study and preservation of the American wilderness. He saw America's rivers, lakes, mountains, and forests as its greatest national treasures, and believed that protecting them from pollution and development was the duty of every American. Through Muir's efforts the U.S. government adopted a policy of preserving and protecting designated areas of wilderness in America as national parks. John Muir is known today as "The Father of National Parks."

Inventor and Activist

Muir has often been regarded as a genius. Although he came from a poor family of Scottish emigrants, he found ways to educate himself, formally and informally, from early youth. By the end of his life Muir had written several authoritative books on wildlife and nature conservation and had been awarded honorary degrees from Yale, Harvard, the University of Wisconsin, and the University of California for his scientific research and progressive achievements as a naturalist. Also a gifted

Considered "The Father of National Parks," John Muir dedicated his life to the study and preservation of the American wilderness.

inventor, Muir patented many ingenious mechanical devices, including a thermometer fashioned from an iron rod, several clocks, and a collapsible bed.

However, Muir is perhaps best known for his campaign to save the forests of the beautiful Yosemite Valley of central California. From his first visit to Yosemite as a young man, he was captivated by its majestic grandeur. For two decades Muir lobbied the federal government for the preservation of Yosemite, wrote numerous magazine articles pleading for its protection, and lectured against destructive grazing and lumbering operations. His appeals galvanized public support for his cause. On October 1, 1890, President Benjamin Harrison signed the bill making Yosemite a national park, and federal troops were assigned to protect the new park from future industrial environmental abuse.

In 1892 Muir helped found the Sierra Club, originally an organization dedicated to enlisting popular and government support for preserving California's Sierra Nevada wilderness. The present-day Sierra Club's dedication to conservation on many fronts manifests John Muir's belief that humanity can redeem itself through its reverence of nature: "No matter into what depths of degradation humanity may sink," Muir once wrote, "I will never despair while the lowest love the pure and the beautiful and know it when they see it."[1]

Although Muir most loved the Sierra Nevada region, his quest to explore remote areas of wilderness led him to make extended travels throughout the United States and to regions as far away as Alaska.

As part of his effort to protect California's Sierra Nevada wilderness, Muir helped found the Sierra Club. Early members of the club are shown in this late-nineteenth-century photo.

Through his writings and public campaigns, Muir brought attention to the need to protect the American wilderness from destruction.

The studies he made during these journeys in botany, zoology, and natural history convinced Muir that there existed a "common purity of Nature."[2] Muir believed that humanity is bound to honor and preserve that natural purity, and this conviction became a guiding principle in his mission to preserve the vanishing wilderness areas of America.

The Legacy of John Muir

John Muir's greatest achievement is the contribution he made to the cause of American forest conservation and wilderness preservation. Through his writings and public campaigns, Muir focused national attention on the necessity of saving public lands for recreation, research, and sanctuary, and of protecting forest reserves from destruction. His eloquent public appeals to halt the accelerating destruction of America's wilderness enlisted the support of private citizens and promi-

nent statesmen, including President Theodore Roosevelt, alike. Indeed, Roosevelt persuaded Congress to create an entire agency, the Bureau of Forestry, to these ends, largely through Muir's efforts.

Muir was a prolific and popular author. In language that may sound quaint to modern ears, he combined scholarly, unembellished description with the ornate, poetic, formal writing style of the day as no nature writer had before. His books are as valuable today as they were nearly one hundred years ago.

The legacy of John Muir is to be found in the splendor of the national parks that he helped create and passionately defended. Muir believed that the beauty of wilderness sanctuaries such as Yosemite Valley would inspire future generations to cherish and protect their natural environment: "The park is the poor man's refuge," John Muir once inscribed in his journal. "Few are altogether blind and deaf to the sweet looks and voices of nature. Everybody at heart loves God's beauty because God made everybody."[3]

1 A Young Lover of Nature

John Muir was born in Dunbar, Scotland, on April 21, 1838. In Scottish dialect the surname Muir means "moor," an uncultivated stretch of wetland. The name appears particularly appropriate for a boy who would grow up to champion the preservation of America's wilderness. In *The Story of My Boyhood and Youth,* one of several autobiographical works, Muir recalls that his love of nature began in early childhood:

> When I was a boy in Scotland, I was fond of everything that was wild, and all my life I've been growing fonder and fonder of wild places and wild creatures. Fortunately around my na-

tive town of Dunbar, by the stormy North Sea, there was no lack of wildness, though most of the land lay in smooth cultivation. My earliest recollections of the country were gained on short walks with my grandfather when I was perhaps not over three years old.[4]

The Muir family—father Daniel, mother Ann Gilrye, John, and his two brothers and four sisters—lived above a store run by Daniel Muir. Despite their father's industriousness the store was not a successful business and the Muir children grew up in poverty. Meals were generally modest portions of oatmeal porridge,

Muir's family lived in the rooms above a store run by Daniel Muir in Dunbar, Scotland. The building was later turned into the hotel pictured.

broth, mutton, potatoes, and tea. From early childhood, Muir developed the lifelong habit of eating very little. Years later in California he would often set out for a day of mountain exploration content with only a few slices of dried bread for his supper.

Boyhood Adventures in Scotland

Even as a child John loved to study. In later years he fondly recalled his excitement while preparing to attend school for the first time:

> I was sent to school before I had completed my third year. The first schoolday was doubtless full of wonders, but I am not able to recall any of them. I remember the servant washing my face and getting soap in my eyes, and mother hanging a little green bag with my first book in it around my neck so I would not lose it, and its blowing back in the sea-wind like a flag. But before I was sent to school my grandfather, as I was told, had taught me my letters from shop signs across the street.

> With my school lessons father made me learn hymns and Bible verses. For learning "Rock of Ages" he gave me a penny, and thus I became suddenly rich. Scotch boys are seldom spoiled with money.[5]

By the time John was eight, he was studying English, Latin, and French as well as arithmetic, history, and geography. Students were required to memorize each day's school lessons and to recite them without error. Schoolteachers of the time applied strict discipline and harsh punishment, whipping any student who failed to deliver a lesson with complete accuracy. The frequency of this punishment left a vivid impression in John's memory. As an adult he would recall that "there was a close connection between the skin and the memory."[6]

The schoolhouse was not the only place where John and his brothers received whippings. Daniel Muir was a stern parent who thrashed his sons for such misbehavior as fighting with other boys or failing to come home before dark. The severity of all this discipline neither embittered John nor daunted his youthful spirits, however.

Many days John and a few companions would brave their parents' displeasure and run off to explore the Scottish countryside. Quite often these excursions would become competitive races, as Muir later recounted:

> A dozen or so of us would start out on races that were simply tests of endurance, running on and on along a public road over the breezy hills like hounds, without stopping or getting tired. The only serious trouble we ever felt in these long races was an occasional stitch in our sides. . . .

> We thought nothing of running right ahead ten or a dozen miles before turning back; for we knew nothing about taking time by the sun, and none of us had a watch in those days. Indeed, we never cared about time until it began to get dark. Then we thought of home and the thrashing that awaited us. Late or early, the thrashing was sure, unless father happened to be away.[7]

A constant outdoor attraction for John and his friends was the great variety of wildlife in the country. John was particularly fascinated with birds and loved to collect abandoned bird nests. He became a careful observer of the habits of the area's robins, skylarks, and sparrows and came to love all winged creatures. Once, as a boy, John nearly wept at the sight of a soldier robbing a robin's nest to sell the young birds at market.

Another of John's favorite pastimes was climbing the high walls of an old abandoned castle near Dunbar with his brother David. The two boys also loved to crawl out of their upper-story bedroom window onto the roof at night after their mother had put them to bed. On one such occasion David found himself stranded on the roof but was afraid to call for help because he feared the whipping he knew would follow as punishment. With great presence of mind, John stood on the windowsill, reached out, grabbed his brother by the feet, and held him securely until David was able to slide back through the window. More than fifty years later Muir revisited his home in Scotland; he describes his reassessment of that childhood adventure in his memoirs:

> I got one of my Dunbar schoolmates to introduce me to the owners of our old home, from whom I obtained permission to go upstairs to examine our bedroom window and judge what sort of adventure getting on its roof must have been, and with all my after experience in mountaineering, I found that what I had done in daring boyhood was now beyond my skill.[8]

These childhood adventures in the Scottish countryside awakened within John a love for adventurous exploration that became a lifelong passion. In his memoirs, Muir remembers this as a magical time:

> Oh, the blessed enchantment of those Saturday runaways in the prime of spring! How our young wondering eyes reveled in the sunny, breezy glory of the hills and the sky, every particle of us thrilling and tingling with the bees and glad birds and glad streams! Kings may be blessed; we were glorious, we were free—school cares and scoldings, heart thrashings and flesh thrashings alike, were forgotten in the fullness of nature's glad wildness. These were my first excursions—the beginning of life-long wanderings.[9]

Sea Voyage to America

When John was eleven years old Daniel Muir sold his store and decided to move his family to America. The announcement that the family was to live in the United States greatly excited young Muir, who looked forward to exploring the woods and mountains of a new country. Preparations for the journey were made quickly. As Muir later recalled:

> Next morning, we went by rail to Glasgow and thence joyfully sailed away from beloved Scotland, flying to our fortunes on the wings of the winds, carefree as thistle seeds. Father took with him only my sister Sarah, (thirteen years of age), myself (eleven), and brother David (nine), leaving my eldest sister Margaret and the three youngest of the family, Daniel, Mary, and Anna, with mother, to join us after a farm had been found in the wilder-

ness and a comfortable house made to receive them.[10]

The Muirs' voyage across the Atlantic to America took six weeks. On their arrival in New York the Muirs were advised by a grain dealer that most of the wheat he handled came from Wisconsin. This convinced Daniel, who intended to raise wheat on a farm, to settle in Wisconsin. He selected a quarter section (a 160-acre tract, one-half mile square) of lake property near Kingston, Wisconsin, which the family named Fountain Lake Farm.

A small shanty constructed of rough bur oak logs stood in the woods on the farm, overlooking a flowery meadow watered by the lake. John was entranced by the beauty of the area and was particularly fond of the meadow. He felt that this lovely grassland should always remain unchanged. Thus Muir's conviction that

A Grandfather's Parting Counsel

Their father's decision to move the family to America was a cause of both elation and sadness for the Muir children. In his book The Story of My Boyhood and Youth, *Muir gives a poignant account of how their youthful excitement was tempered by the wise advice of their grandfather.*

"One night, when David and I were at grandfather's fireside solemnly learning our lessons as usual, my father came in with news, the most wonderful, most glorious, that wild boys ever heard. 'Bairns' he said, 'you needna learn your lessons the nicht, for we're gan to America the morn!' No more grammar, but boundless woods full of mysterious good things; trees full of sugar, growing in ground full of gold; hawks, eagles, pigeons, filling the sky; millions of birds' nests, and no gamekeepers to stop us in all the wild, happy land. We were utterly, blindly glorious. After father left the room, grandfather gave David and me a gold coin apiece for a keepsake, and looked very serious, for he was about to be deserted in his lonely old age. And when we in fullness of young joy spoke of what we were going to do, of the wonderful birds and their nests that we should find, the sugar and gold, etc. and promised to send him a big box full of that tree sugar packed in gold from the glorious paradise over the sea, poor lonely grandfather, about to be forsaken, looked with downcast eyes on the floor and said in a low, trembling, troubled voice, 'Ah, poor laddies, poor laddies, you'll find something else ower the sea forbye gold and sugar, birds' nests and freedom fra lessons and schools. You'll find plenty hard, hard work.' And so we did."

Muir's sketch of the house his father built on the Fountain Lake Farm in Wisconsin. The beauty of the area, which included a lake and flowery meadows, led Muir to the belief that certain areas of wilderness should be permanently protected.

certain tracts of land should be set aside to be protected permanently as wilderness regions took its first form.

A Youth of Grim Hardship

John found little time to explore the woodlands and meadows of his new home, however. His father was a stern taskmaster who demanded that his sons work at least sixteen hours a day cultivating the farmland and otherwise laboring. Although the boys were not permitted to attend school, John persuaded his father to allow him to continue his study of mathematics and literature with the few books he was able to borrow from neighbors, and to read early in the morning before the workday began.

The arduous work of completely clearing the land and cultivating the fields of Fountain Lake Farm took eight years. During that time the elder Muir continued to impose harsh physical discipline. While

they lived in his household he demanded their complete submission to a life of humble labor. Recalling his father's tyranny, Muir later wrote:

> Strange to say, father carefully taught us to consider ourselves very poor worms of the dust . . . and devoutly believed that quenching every spark of pride and self-confidence was a sacred duty, without realizing that in so doing he might at the same time be quenching everything else. Praise he considered most venomous, and tried to assure me that when I was fairly out in the wicked world making my own way I would soon learn that although I might have thought him a hard taskmaster at times, strangers were far harder. On the contrary, I found no lack of kindness and sympathy.[11]

Daniel Muir was so encouraged by the successful development of Fountain Lake Farm that he purchased an additional 320 acres of wildland, committing himself and his sons to more years of work clearing the property for another farm, which he named Hickory Hill. John was assigned the hazardous task of digging a well for the farm. At one point in the excavation, he hit a pocket of carbonic acid gas and would have suffocated had he not managed to shout out an alarm calling his father to his rescue.

As he grew older the severity of John's home life made the woods all the more an escape where he could seek refuge in the beauty of the nearby forests and glades. John's love of birds flourished. He delighted in discovering the abundant variety of species that thrived in the Wisconsin woods. Whenever he lingered too long on these wanderings, he faced the inevitable whipping upon his return home with quiet obedience. But as John approached young manhood he made up his mind to leave the family farm and strike out on his own.

A Gift for Invention

In 1860 Muir was twenty-two years old and ready to venture out on his own as an adult. He had discovered that he possessed a talent for building mechanical devices and had already developed a number of ingenious inventions. One remarkable early achievement was the assembly of the Muir family's first clock. Although Muir had never seen the inner workings of a clock, reasoning led him to propose its operation. Devising a system using rocks for weights, wheels, and a chain, he managed to build an impressive clock, which the family proudly displayed in their parlor. The clock kept good time and struck a tone on the hour.

The success of this first timepiece encouraged Muir to build other clocks. He also fashioned a large thermometer from an iron rod that he had taken from an old wagon box. Muir discovered that the metal rod would expand when heated and contract as it cooled. Measuring the degrees of contraction with a series of iron levers, Muir devised a temperature gauge with a dial that responded to the slightest change in the size of the rod.

Neighbors were impressed by Muir's inventions and encouraged him to display them at the state fair at Madison, Wisconsin. As Muir prepared to leave for Madison, Daniel gave him advice that he later recalled with a degree of humor and regret:

A sketch from one of Muir's notebooks shows his ingenious plans for a thermometer.

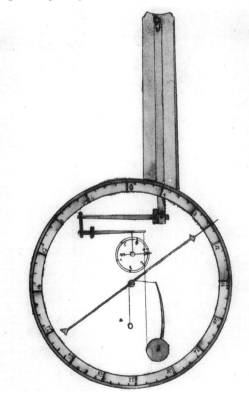

Invented by Muir while at college, this desk had a built-in clock and gears that moved one book aside and the next into place after a designated amount of study time.

When I told father that I was about to leave home, and inquired whether, if I should happen to be in need of money, he would send me a little he said, "No; depend entirely on yourself." Good advice, I suppose, but surely needlessly severe for so bashful, home-loving a boy who had worked so hard. I had the gold sovereign that my grandfather had given me when I left Scotland, and a few dollars, perhaps ten, that I had made by raising a few

bushels of grain on a little patch of sandy abandoned ground. So when I left home to try the world I had only about fifteen dollars in my pocket.[12]

Traveling on foot, Muir set out for Madison in September 1860. "All the baggage I carried," he later recalled, "was a package made up of the two clocks and a small thermometer made of a piece of old washboard, all tied together."[13] His inventions attracted attention immediately upon his arrival, and his exhibits soon became the most popular displayed at the fair. Several newspaper accounts were published and he was awarded a prize of fifteen dollars for his inventions.

Endeavors in Self-Reliance

Although he was pleased by this recognition, Muir had resolved that his primary ambition was to continue his education. After attending a preparatory school for a few weeks, he entered the University of Wisconsin. He worked his way through college for the next four years. True to his father's parting advice, Muir remained entirely self-reliant and supported himself during his college career. As he recounts:

During the four years that I was in the University, I earned enough in the harvest-fields during the long summer vacations to carry me through the balance of each year, working very hard, cutting with a cradle four acres of wheat a day, and helping to put it in the shock. But having to buy books and paying I think, thirty-dollars a year for instruction, and occasionally buying acids and retorts, glass tubing, bell-

A Childhood Garden

Muir's fascination with the science of botany began with a childhood love of plants and flowers. The family garden was regarded as one of the household's great treasures, as he recalls in The Story of My Boyhood and Youth.

"Father was proud of his garden and seemed always to be trying to make it as much like Eden as possible, and in a corner of it he gave each of us a little bit of ground for our very own in which we planted what we best liked, wondering how the hard dry seeds could change into soft leaves and flowers and find their way out into the light; and, to see how they were coming on, we used to dig up the larger ones, such as peas, beans every day. My aunt had a corner assigned to her in our garden which she filled with lilies, and we all looked with the utmost respect and admiration at that precious lily-bed and wondered whether when we grew up we should ever be rich enough to own anything like so grand. We imagined that each lily was worth an enormous sum of money and never dared to touch a single leaf or petal of them. We really stood in awe of them. Far, far was I then from the wild lily gardens of California that I was destined to see in their glory."

glasses, flasks, etc., I had to cut down expenses for board now and then to half a dollar a week.

One winter I taught school ten miles south of Madison, earning much-needed money at the rate of twenty dollars a month, boarding round [working for room and board], and keeping up my University work studying at night.[14]

In addition to working as a school-teacher, Muir managed to sell some of his inventions to finance his education. One of the most popular was a collapsible bed that was attached by a system of levers to a clock. The bed was engineered in such a

An 1861 photo of Muir during his days as a student at the University of Wisconsin. To meet his expenses while at the university, Muir taught school and sold his unique mechanical inventions.

way that at a specific time the clock's mechanism would trigger the bed to tip the person sleeping in it upright and deposit him or her on the floor.

The combined income from the sale of these items and job wages provided Muir with adequate funds to finance his college education, and he diligently applied himself to his studies. One of his instructors, a professor of geology named Ezra Carr, became an important influence on Muir at the university; Muir remained close friends with both Professor Carr and his wife, Jeanne, for many years. In Carr's classes Muir was introduced to the theory of glaciation advanced by the Swiss naturalist Louis Agassiz. Based on Agassiz's research in the Swiss Alps, the theory asserted that the earth had passed through an ice age when an immense ice sheet flowed south from the North Pole to central Europe and Asia. According to Agassiz, the ice flow cut huge passages through solid rock and excavated deep canyons and lake beds as it moved across the continents. Muir was greatly impressed by this theory. It provoked in him a life-long fascination with glaciers that would influence his work as a naturalist in later years.

Before completing his final year at the university, Muir was overtaken by restlessness and a desire to travel. He decided to leave college without taking a degree and set out to explore the Canadian wilderness. At Meaford, Canada, Muir obtained a job with a company that manufactured handles for brooms and rakes. He soon impressed his employers by improving the machinery that produced these handles, making the process completely automatic. Unfortunately, the factory caught fire one night and burned to the ground. Muir then made his way to Indianapolis to work for a carriage parts manufacturer, Osgood, Smith & Company. There also Muir proved himself an asset by improving production methods. He was promoted to foreman and promised a partnership in the company. His future bright, Muir appeared destined at this point to a career as a mechanical inventor. A strange accident, however, would drastically change the direction of his life.

A New Vision

Recorded in The Life and Letters of John Muir *is Muir's reaction to regaining his eyesight after an accident temporarily blinded him.*

"As soon as I got out into Heaven's light I started on another long excursion, making haste with all my heart to store my mind with the Lord's beauty and thus be ready for any fate, light or dark. And it was from this time that my long continuous wanderings may be said to have fairly commenced. I bade adieu to all my mechanical inventions, determined to devote the rest of my life to the study of the inventions of God."

Ezra Carr, one of Muir's professors at college, introduced Muir to the theory of glaciation, an idea that would begin Muir's lifelong fascination with glaciers.

Blindness and a New Vision

One day while Muir was unlacing a belt used to drive the shaft of a machine, the file he was using to remove the stitches in the leather suddenly slipped and pierced his right eye. Muir temporarily lost the sight in that eye and soon after became completely blind when his left eyesight failed in sympathetic blindness with the injured right eye. The grief-stricken Muir feared that he would never again see the brilliant colors of such natural delights as wildflowers, sunsets, and brightly plumed birds. He resolved that should his vision return he would leave the world of industry and mechanical invention and instead seek his life's calling in the wilderness among the trees, mountains, lakes, and wildlife that Muir came to regard as the "inventions of God."[15] Fortunately, the blindness proved to be temporary and Muir eventually regained his sight. When he was well enough to travel, he returned to the outdoors with a goal: to undertake a cross-country journey southward on foot to see the wildlife and vegetation of the southeastern United States. Muir would later write about this southbound journey in his book *A Thousand Mile Walk to the Gulf.* Though he did not anticipate it, these first steps would culminate in recognition of his status as America's greatest conservationist.

2 "John Muir, Earth-Planet, Universe"

When he had recovered from the accident to his eye, Muir returned to Wisconsin to visit his family and begin preparations for his extensive field trip south. He was especially keen to observe the various plant life of the countryside through which he would travel. While attending the University of Wisconsin another student had introduced Muir, always fascinated with flowers and other plants, to the science of botany. Muir later recorded the incident vividly in his memoirs:

I received my first lesson in botany from a student by the name of Griswold, who is now County Judge of the County of Waukesha, Wisconsin. . . . One memorable day in June, when I was standing on the stone steps of the north dormitory, Mr. Griswold joined me and at once began to teach. He reached up, plucked a flower from an overspreading branch of a locust tree, and, handing it to me, said, "Muir, do you know what family this tree belongs to?"

An Early View of Ecology

As a young man Muir developed a belief that all living things on earth are interrelated. This conviction remained with him throughout his life as it was expressed in A Thousand Mile Walk to the Gulf.

"Now, it never seems to occur to these far-seeing teachers that Nature's object in making animals and plants might possibly be first of all the happiness of each one of them, not the creation of all for the happiness of one. Why should man value himself as more than a small part of the one great unit of creation? And what creature of all that the Lord has taken the pains to make is not essential to the completeness of that unit—the cosmos? The universe would be incomplete without man; but it would also be incomplete without the smallest transmicroscopic creature that dwells beyond our conceitful eyes and knowledge."

"No," I said, "I don't know anything about botany."

"Well, no matter," said he, "what is it like?"

"It's like a pea flower," I replied.

"That's right. You're right," he said, "it belongs to the Pea Family."

"But how can that be," I objected, "when the pea is a weak, clinging, straggling herb, and the locust a big, thorny hardwood tree?"

"Yes, that is true," he replied, "as to the difference in size, but it is also true that in all their essential characters they are alike, and therefore they must belong to one and the same family."[16]

Griswold then pointed out to Muir the similarity in the shapes of the upper and lower petals of the flowers of both the pea and the locust tree, and the fact that the seeds of both are contained in pods. He instructed Muir to taste the leaves of both the pea and the locust tree; they were similar in flavor as well. Griswold concluded his lecture with a compelling statement:

Now, surely you cannot imagine that all these similar characters are mere coincidences. Do they not rather go to show that the Creator in making the pea vine and locust tree had the same idea in mind, and that plants are not classified arbitrarily? Man has nothing to do with their classification. Nature has attended to all that, giving essential unity with boundless variety, so that the botanist has only to examine plants to learn the harmony of their relations.[17]

The lesson introduced Muir to an entirely new dimension of biology that was to influence his entire life:

This fine lesson charmed me and sent me flying to the woods and meadows in wild enthusiasm. Like everybody else I was always fond of flowers, attracted by their external beauty and purity. Now my eyes opened to their inner beauty, all alike revealing glorious traces of the thoughts of God, and leading on and on into the infinite cosmos.[18]

A Thousand-Mile Walk to the Gulf of Mexico

Muir had decided to walk south across America and on into South America to study the tropical flowers of that region. On September 1, 1867, he bade his parents farewell and boarded a train to Louisville, Kentucky, the stepping-off point for his thousand-mile journey to Florida and the Gulf of Mexico. He was twenty-nine years old.

Muir had decided to keep a written account of his travels. On the front page of his journal he inscribed the words "John Muir, Earth-Planet, Universe." His only possessions were a wooden press for collecting plants, a small rubber bag containing a change of underwear, towel, comb, and brush, and three books: a copy of the New Testament, Milton's *Paradise Lost*, and a volume of poetry by fellow Scot Robert Burns. Recalling this adventure years later, Muir wrote: "When I set out on the long excursion that finally led to California, I wandered, afoot and alone, from Indiana to the Gulf of Mexico with a plant press on my back, holding a generally southward course, like the birds when they are going from summer to winter."[19]

At the age of twenty-nine, Muir embarked on an incredible thousand-mile walk from Louisville, Kentucky, to the Gulf of Mexico. Along the way Muir recorded his observations in a journal inscribed "John Muir, Earth-Planet, Universe."

Avoiding Bandits

Muir made his way across country, sometimes eating meals with families of farmers who invited him to share their breakfast or supper, often sleeping contently outdoors when there was no bed available. What little money he carried paid for his food and a bed for the night when sleeping in the open was risky. The Civil War had ended two years earlier and the South was filled with displaced people and va-

grants, many lawless. Wary of robbers, Muir made cautious attempts to avoid bandits. One afternoon he found himself confronted by ten horsemen on a mountain road. He writes:

> Toward sundown, as I was walking rapidly along a straight stretch in the road, I suddenly came in sight of ten mounted men riding abreast. They undoubtedly had seen me before I had discovered them, for they had stopped their horses and were evidently watching me.
>
> I knew that there was nothing for it but to face them fearlessly, without showing the slightest suspicion of foul play. Therefore, without halting even for a moment, I advanced rapidly with long strides as though I intended to walk through the midst of them. Stopping never an instant, I turned to one side and walked around them to get on the road again, and kept on without venturing to look back or to betray the slightest fear of being robbed.
>
> After I had gone about one hundred or one hundred and fifty yards, I ventured a quick glance back, without stopping, and saw in this flash of an eye that all the ten had turned their horses toward me and were evidently talking about me; supposedly, with reference to what my object was, where I was going, and whether it would be worth while to rob me.
>
> Evidently they belonged to the most irreclaimable of the guerrilla [outlaw] bands who, long accustomed to plunder, deplored the coming of peace. I was not followed, however, probably because the plants projecting from my

plant press made them believe that I was a poor herb doctor, a common occupation in these mountain regions.[20]

Muir's travels took him across both the Cumberland and Blue Ridge ranges of the Appalachian Mountains. He was enthralled by the great variety of grasses, flowers, trees, and other plant life he observed along the way. Each day seemed to reveal to Muir new botanical discoveries, which he recorded with enthusiasm and careful detail in his journal:

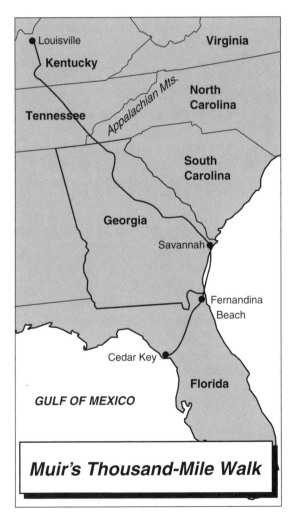

Muir's Thousand-Mile Walk

28 September: The water oak is abundant on stream banks and in damp hollows. Grasses are becoming tall and cane-like and do not cover the ground with their leaves as at the North. Strange plants are crowding about me now. Scarce a familiar face appears among all the flowers of the day's walk.

29 September: Today I met a magnificent grass, ten or twelve feet in stature, with a superb panicle [branch of flowers] of glossy purple flowers. Its leaves, too, are of princely mould and dimensions. Its home is in sunny meadows and along the wet borders of slow streams and swamps. It seems to be fully aware of its high rank, and waves with the grace and solemn majesty of a mountain pine. I wish I could place one of these regal plants among the grass settlements of our Western prairies. Surely every panicle would wave and bow in joyous allegiance and acknowledge their king.[21]

A Strange Campsite

Muir reached Savannah, Georgia, on October 8, 1867, expecting to find a sum of money from his brother waiting at the post office there. To Muir's disappointment the money had not yet arrived, so he spent his first night in town in the cheapest lodging house that he could find.

When the money failed to arrive the next day, Muir sought but could not find work in the town. With only a dollar and a half in his pocket, Muir knew that he could not afford to continue boarding in the lodging house. Budgeting his money by allotting a few cents a day for a little bread or a few crackers, Muir decided to search for a secluded place where he could camp until the funds arrived. His search led him to a cemetery known as the Bonaventure graveyard. In *A Thousand Mile Walk to the Gulf,* Muir recalls his decision to seek shelter in the graveyard:

> I wandered wearily from dune to dune sinking ankle-deep in the sand, searching for a place to sleep beneath the tall flowers, free from insects and snakes, and above all from my fellow man. But idle negroes were prowling about everywhere, and I was afraid.

Muir kept detailed accounts of his travels and wrote many letters to friends and family while away. A self-portrait from one of his letters is pictured.

The wind had strange sounds, waving the heavy panicles over my head, and I feared sickness from malaria so prevalent here, when suddenly I thought of the graveyard.

"There," thought I, "is an ideal place for a penniless wanderer. There no superstitious prowling mischief maker dares venture for fear of haunting ghosts, while for me there will be God's rest and peace. And then, if I am to be exposed to unhealthy vapours, I shall have capital compensation in seeing those grand oaks in the moonlight, with all the impressive and nameless influences of this lonely beautiful place."[22]

"A Jubilee of Bread"

Muir spent five nights camping in the cemetery waiting for the money from his brother to reach him. During the day he continued to look for work, without success. His money was quickly running out and he was growing desperate. As he walked to town on the sixth morning after his arrival, the ground before Muir seemed to rise up in front of him and he realized that he was dangerously hungry. To his great relief, the money was waiting. In his memoirs Muir recalls how he relished the first substantial food he had eaten in days:

> Gladly I pocketed the money, and had not gone along the street more than a few rods [1 rod equals 5.5 yards] before I met a very large negro woman with a tray of gingerbread, in which I immediately invested some of my new

Georgia Hospitality

Muir particularly enjoyed his encounters with the people of Georgia. In A Thousand Mile Walk to the Gulf, *Muir includes a highly complimentary description of these people.*

"Of the people of the States that I have now passed, I best liked the Georgians. They have charming manners, and their dwellings are mostly larger and better than those of adjacent States. However costly or ornamental their homes or their manners, they do not, like those of the New Englander, appear as the fruits of intense and painful sacrifice and training, but are entirely divested of artificial weights and measures, and seem to pervade and twine about their characters as spontaneous growths with the durability and charm of living nature."

wealth, and walked rejoicingly, munching along the street, making no attempt to conceal the pleasure I had in eating. Then, still hunting for more food, I found a sort of eating-place in a market and had a large regular meal on top of the gingerbread! Thus my "marching through Georgia" terminated handsomely in a jubilee of bread.[23]

A Floral Pilgrimage

His finances improved, Muir was anxious to continue what he called his "floral pilgrimage."[24] Departing Savannah he traveled by boat to northern Florida. On October 15 he landed at the town of Fernandina, Florida, and recorded the event with great emotion in his journal:

Today, at last I reached Florida, the so-called "Land of Flowers," that I had so long waited for, wondering if after all my longings and prayers would be in vain, and I should die without a glimpse of the watery, reedy coast, with clumps of mangrove and forests of moss-dressed, strange trees appearing low in the distance.[25]

The swamps and marshes Muir described in his journal were infested with malaria-bearing mosquitoes. Despite apprehensions about health risks, Muir walked west through these swamplands, so to reach Florida's west coast, the Gulf of Mexico, and Cuba. There Muir's plans to continue his botanical journey into South America changed, as he explains in his memoirs:

From the west coat of Florida I crossed the gulf to Cuba, enjoyed the rich tropical flora there for a few months, intending to go thence to the north end of South America, make my way through the woods to the headwaters of the Amazon, and float down that

Great Expectations

Muir's arrival in Florida proved to be somewhat of a disappointment to him. His first view of the state was dramatically different from what he had expected, as he recalls in A Thousand Mile Walk to the Gulf.

"In visiting Florida in dreams, of either day or night, I always came suddenly on a close forest of trees, every one in flower, and bent down and entangled to network by luxuriant, bright blooming vines, and over all a flood of bright sunlight. But such was not the gate by which I entered the promised land. Salt marshes, belonging more to the sea than land; with groves here and there, green and unflowered, sunk to the shoulders in sedges and rushes; with trees farther back, ill defined in their boundary, and instead of rising in hilly waves and swellings, stretching inland in low water-like levels."

grand river to the ocean. But I was unable to find a ship bound for South America—fortunately perhaps, for I had incredibly little money for so long a trip and had not yet fully recovered from a fever caught in the Florida swamps. Therefore I decided to visit California for a year or two to see its wonderful flora and the famous Yosemite Valley. All the world was before me and everyday was a holiday, so it did not seem important to which one of the world's wilderness I first should wander.[26]

Muir's high spirits over the prospect of exploring new regions in California overrode his disappointment over the aborted South American trip. On March 10, 1868, Muir took passage on a ship bound for the Isthmus of Panama. From there he traveled overland by train to the Pacific coast and boarded a ship for California. The journey upon which Muir embarked would lead him to a land he later described as "glowing golden in the sunshine," and to a valley he was destined to cherish and defend for the rest of his life.[27]

Chapter

3 "The Range of Light"

The Panama steamer on which Muir had booked passage arrived in San Francisco on March 28, 1868. Muir was eager to explore the California countryside and spent only one day in the city. As he walked down the street, Muir stopped a man and asked him "for the nearest way out of town." When the startled passerby asked him where he wished to go, Muir replied: "To any place that is wild."[28] Following directions to take the Oakland Ferry across the bay, Muir set out on foot eastward, into the lower ranges of the Sierra Nevada, towards the Yosemite Valley.

First View of the Sierras

It was spring and the grasslands and foothills through which he traveled were covered with wildflowers. One morning after climbing an elevation called Pacheco Pass, Muir stood on the summit of the hill and gazed down at a wide grassy valley with a majestic wall of mountains to the east.

Years later he recounted in vivid detail his first view of the Sierra Nevada:

At my feet lay the Great Central Valley [San Joaquin Valley] of California, level and flowery, like a lake of pure sunshine, forty or fifty miles wide, five

hundred miles long, one rich furred garden of yellow *Compositae*. And from the eastern boundary of this vast golden flower-bed rose the mighty Sierra, miles in height, and so gloriously coloured and so radiant, it seemed not clothed with light, but wholly composed of it, like the wall of some celestial city. Along the top and extending a good way down, was a rich pearl-grey belt of snow; below it a belt of blue and dark purple, marking the extension of the forests; and stretching along the base of the range a broad belt of rose-purple; all these colours, from the blue sky to the yellow valley smoothly blending as they do in a rainbow, making a wall of light ineffably fine. Then it seemed to me that the Sierra should be called, not the Nevada or Snowy Range, but the Range of Light.[29]

Muir descended Pacheco Pass, continued his journey across the San Joaquin Valley, and began his ascent into the Sierra Nevada toward Yosemite Valley. As he climbed the foothills toward the higher mountain ranges, Muir made careful notes of the land's geographical features. In his memoirs he describes these first impressions of the Sierra Nevada:

A Memorable Trek

Upon his arrival in California, Muir and a companion set out on foot across the San Joaquin Valley to the Sierra Nevada. William Frederic Badè includes this account of the experience in The Life and Letters of John Muir.

"Both my companion and myself had lived on common air for nearly thirty years, and never before this discovered that our bodies contained such multitudes of plates, or that this mortal flesh, so little valued by philosophers and teachers, was possessed of so vast a capacity for happiness.

We were new creatures, born again; and truly not until this time were we fairly conscious that we were born at all. Never more, thought I as we strode forward at faster speed, never more shall I sentimentalize about getting free from the flesh, for it is steeped like a sponge in immortal pleasure."

Were we to cross-cut the Sierra Nevada into blocks a dozen miles or so to thickness, each section would contain a Yosemite Valley and a river, together with a bright array of lakes and meadows, rocks and forests. The grandeur and inexhaustible beauty of each block would be so vast and over-satisfying that to choose among them would be like selecting slices of bread cut from the same loaf. One bread-slice might have burnt spots, answering to craters; another would be more browned; another, more crusted or raggedly-cut, but all essentially the same.[30]

Muir was particularly impressed by an oval-shaped valley called Twenty Hill Hollow, situated between the Merced and Tuolumne Rivers. Approximately a mile in length, Twenty Hill Hollow was named for the twenty rounded hills that formed the banks of the valley. Muir found this valley exceptionally beautiful and later recorded his impressions of the Hollow:

> Its twenty hills are as wonderfully regular in size and position as in form. They are like big marbles half buried in the ground, each poised and settled daintily into its place at a regular distance from its fellows, making a charming fairy-land of hills, with small, grassy valleys between, each valley having a tiny stream of its own, which leaps and sparkles out into the open hollow, uniting to form Hollow Creek.[31]

The Grandeur of Yosemite

As Muir approached the higher elevations of the mountains, the air cooled and he found patches of snow on the ground. The terrain gradually changed from grasslands to lush forests filled with a wide variety of trees. Muir writes fondly:

> Sauntering up the foothills to Yosemite by any of the old trails or roads in use before the railway was built from the town of Merced up the river to the boundary of Yosemite Park, richer and wilder become the forests and streams. At elevation of 6,000 ft. above the level of the sea the silver firs are 200 ft. high, with branches whorled around the colossal shafts in regular order, and every branch beautifully primate like a fern frond. The Douglas spruce, the yellow and sugar pines and brown-barked Libocedrus here reached their finest developments of beauty and grandeur. The majestic Sequoia is here, too, the king of conifers, the noblest of all the noble race.[32]

Muir was captivated by the grandeur of Yosemite and considered the valley, with its lush forests, waterfalls, and domed peaks to be among the most beautiful places he had ever visited.

His anticipation growing, Muir continued through the woods toward Yosemite Valley. Finally, emerging from the forests into a clearing overlooking the valley, Muir enjoyed his first view of the magnificent Yosemite:

The most famous and accessible of these canyon valleys, and also the one that presents their most striking and sublime features on the grandest scale, is the Yosemite, situated in the basin of the Merced River at an elevation of 4000 feet above the level of the sea. It is about seven miles long, half a mile to a mile wide, and nearly a mile deep in the solid granite flank of the range. The walls are made up of rocks, mountains in size, partly separated from each other by side canyons, and they are so sheer in front, and so compactly and harmoniously arranged on a level floor, that the Valley, comprehensively seen, looks like an immense hall or temple lighted from above. . . .

Down through the middle of the Valley flows the crystal Merced, River of Mercy, peacefully quiet, reflecting lilies and trees and the onlooking rocks; things frail and fleeting and types of endurance meeting here and blending in countless forms, as if into this one mountain mansion Nature had gathered her choicest treasures, to draw her lovers into close and confiding communion with her.[33]

Muir grew to love Yosemite Valley more than any other place. The valley's great beauty inspired in Muir love of the earth in all its complexity and faith in the laws of nature. During his early wanderings in the Sierra Nevada, Muir described these feelings in his journal:

If my soul could get away from this so-called prison [the human body], be granted all the list of attributes generally bestowed on spirits, my first ramble on spirit wings would not be among the volcanoes of the moon. Nor should I follow the sunbeams to their source in the sun. I should hover about the beauty of our own good star [Earth]. . . . I should study Nature's laws in all their crossings and unions; I should follow magnetic streams to their source, and follow the shores of our magnetic oceans. . . . And I should go to the very center of our globe and read the whole splendid page from the beginning. . . .

But my first journeys would be into the inner substance of flowers, and among the folds and mazes of Yosemite's falls.[34]

Muir spent ten days in the mountains, meadows, and rivers of the Sierra Nevada, living on a frugal diet of bread and tea. When his provisions were exhausted, Muir reluctantly departed the mountains and returned to the foothills to look for work. But his exploration of Yosemite Valley was to become the work of a lifetime. In 1912, more than forty years after his first visit to the Sierra Nevada, Muir published *The Yosemite*, a carefully researched natural history of the valley. His passionate advocacy for its preservation grew out of his intimate knowledge of the place and the life in it.

First Mountain Excursion

For the rest of 1868 Muir worked at a number of jobs, herding sheep and gentling wild horses, looking for ways to return to the mountains. In early June 1869

Visitors ride a horse-pulled carriage through a wooded Yosemite trail.

an Irish sheep rancher named Pat Delaney offered Muir a job that provided him with an ideal opportunity to return to Yosemite. As Muir gratefully recalls:

> I was longing for the mountains about this time, but money was scarce and I couldn't see how a bread supply was to be kept up. . . .
>
> Mr. Delaney, a sheep-owner, for whom I worked a few weeks, called on me and offered to engage me to go with his shepherd and flock to the headwaters of the Merced and Tuolumne Rivers—the very region I had most in mind. I was in the mood to accept work of any kind that would take me into the mountains whose treasures I had tasted last summer in the Yosemite region. The flock, he explained, would be moved gradually higher through the successive forest belts as the snow melted, stopping for a few weeks at the best places we came to. These I thought would be good centres of observation from which I might be able to make many telling excursions within a radius of eight or ten miles of the camps to learn something of the plants, animals and rocks; for he assured me that I should be left perfectly free to follow my studies.[35]

Muir spent six weeks in the high mountains assisting the shepherd with his flock. He spent his free time there happily exploring, making black-and-white sketches of the scenery, and recording observations in his journal:

28 June. Warm mellow summer. The glowing sunbeams make every nerve tingle. The new needles of the pines and firs are nearly full grown and shine gloriously.[36]

1 July. Summer is ripe. Flocks of seeds are already out of their cups and pods seeking their predestined places. . . . I like to watch the squirrels. There are two species here, the large California grey and the Douglas. The latter is the brightest of all the squirrels I have ever seen, a hot spark of life.[37]

27 July. Up and away to Lake Tenaya—another big day, enough for a lifetime. . . . Beyond the silver firs I find the two-leaved pine (*Pinus contorta,* var. *Murrayanna*) forms the bulk of the forest up to an elevation of ten thousand feet or more—the highest timber-belt of the Sierra.[38]

One of the more memorable incidents recorded in Muir's journal was his encounter with a bear while rambling through the woods:

He [the bear] made a telling picture standing alert in the sunny forest garden. . . .

I thought I should like to see his gait in running, so I made a sudden rush at him, shouting and swinging my hat to frighten him, expecting to see him

Sheep graze in the Tuolumne meadows. As an assistant to a sheepherder in Yosemite, Muir was able to spend time exploring the high mountains.

A Rainstorm's Rhapsody

Muir's intense love of nature was often expressed in poetic writing. In his book My First Summer in the Sierra *Muir recounts his experiences during a thunderstorm while in the mountains.*

"How fiercely, devoutly wild is Nature in the midst of her beauty-loving tenderness!—painting lilies, watering them, caressing them with gentle hand, going from flower to flower like a gardener while building rock mountains and cloud mountains full of lightning and rain. Gladly we run for shelter beneath an overhanging cliff and examine the reassuring ferns and mosses, gentle love tokens growing in cracks and chinks. . . . To these one's heart goes home, and the voices of the storm become gentle. Now the sun breaks forth and fragrant steam arises. The birds are out singing on the edges of the grove. The west is flaming in gold and purple, ready for the ceremony of the sunset, and back I go to camp with my notes and pictures, the best of them printed in my mind as dreams. A fruitful day, without measured beginning or ending. A terrestrial eternity. A gift of good God."

make haste to get away. But to my dismay he did not run or show any sign of running. On the contrary, he stood his ground ready to fight and defend himself, lowered his head, thrust it forward, and looked sharply and fiercely at me. Then I suddenly began to fear that upon me would fall the work of running. . . .

How long our awfully strenuous interview lasted, I don't know; but at length in the slow fullness of time he pulled his huge paws down off the log, with magnificent deliberation turned and walked leisurely up the meadow, stopping frequently to look back over his shoulder to see whether I was pursuing him, then moving on back again, evidently neither fearing me very much nor trusting me.[39]

As autumn approached, Muir reluctantly made preparations to break camp and drive the sheep flock back down to Delaney's ranch in the San Joaquin Valley. He had felt at home in the mountain wilderness and vowed to himself that he would return soon. On September 22, 1869, Muir made his final entry in the journal he would later publish as the book *My First Summer in the Sierra:*

> Here ends my forever memorable first High Sierra excursion. I have crossed the Range of Light, surely the brightest and best of all the Lord has built; and rejoicing in its glory, I gladly, hopefully, pray I may see it again.[40]

4 Early Explorations (1869–1874)

Muir's great enjoyment of his first lengthy excursion into the Sierras strengthened his conviction that he would always be happiest living in the wilderness. At the same time he was faced with the necessity of earning a living. Following his return from the mountains Muir worked for several weeks at various odd jobs on Pat Delaney's ranch but in November 1869 he decided to return to Yosemite. Accompanied by a young acquaintance from Philadelphia, Harry Randall, Muir traveled to a hotel near Yosemite Falls and applied to the hotel's owner, James M. Hutchings, for work.

In 1869 Muir was offered a job as tour guide for guests staying at this Yosemite hotel. The owner of the hotel also gave him a job operating a sawmill on the property, allowing Muir to live in the wilderness and earn a living.

Muir's sketch of the cabin he and a friend built for themselves in Yosemite. Muir called the cabin, which overlooked Yosemite Falls, "the handsomest building in the valley."

Hutchings agreed to hire both men. Randall was employed to milk cows and herd oxen, and Muir was hired to build and operate a sawmill on the property. Muir and Randall first built themselves a cabin on the sunny north side of Yosemite Valley and furnished it with a table, bookcase, bench, and hammock beds. The cabin's single window opened on a beautiful view of Yosemite Falls, and Muir later described the shelter as "the handsomest building in the valley."[41]

James Hutchings shared John Muir's love for the Sierra forests, and their employment contract specified that no living trees would be felled for lumber. In 1867 a great storm had uprooted more than a hundred huge pine trees in the valley and the two men agreed that the already fallen timber would be sufficient to supply Hutchings's sawmill. When their cabin was finished, Muir set to work constructing the mill and installing the necessary equipment. In addition to these responsi-

bilities, he was often required to serve as tour guide for many of the hotel's guests.

Exploring Yosemite

Despite his many duties, on Sundays Muir was free to continue his rambles through the forests and meadows of Yosemite Valley. Often accompanied by Randall, he would embark on what he later recalled as "a good Sabbath day's journey," exploring the nearer canyons and ravines.[42] During these wanderings Muir frequented two favorite observation points that provided him with sweeping views of Yosemite Valley.

The first location was the high granite elevation of Sentinel Dome. From this point, Muir could study the courses of the Tuolumne and Merced Rivers. Muir's second observatory was located on a ledge on the north wall east of Yosemite Falls called Sunnyside Bench. From this location, Muir

While working in Yosemite, Muir used his free time to explore the forests and meadows in the area. One of his favorite observation points was atop Sentinel Dome (pictured), where he could study the courses of the rivers that ran below.

could survey the main valley and all its geographical features. Nearly forty years after he made these one-day excursions, Muir recommended a visit to Sentinel Dome to readers of his book *The Yosemite:*

> If I were so time-poor as to have only one day to spend in Yosemite I should start at daybreak, say at three o'clock in midsummer, with a pocketful of any sort of dry breakfast stuff, for Glacier Point, Sentinel Dome, the head of Illilouette Fall, Nevada Fall, the top of Liberty Gap, Vernal Fall and the wild boulder-choked River Canyon. . . .

At an elevation of about five hundred feet a particularly fine, wide-sweeping view down the Valley is obtained, past the sheer face of the Sentinel and between the Cathedral Rocks and El Capitan (granite cliffs). . . .

The views from the summit of Sentinel Dome are still more extensive and telling. Eastward the crowds of peaks at the head of the Merced, Tuolumne and San Joaquin Rivers are presented in bewildering array; westward, the vast forests, yellow foothills and the broad San Joaquin plains and the Coast Ranges, hazy and dim in the distance.[43]

In May of 1870 James Hutchings returned to Yosemite after an extended business trip to San Francisco, and relieved Muir of the responsibility of serving as the hotel's tour guide. Hutchings directed Muir to focus all of his attention on the operation of the sawmill. Muir's somewhat reduced workload and his efficiency in the sawmill left him with many free hours to continue his explorations of the Sierra.

A Compelling Theory

During his mountain excursions, Muir observed many rock formations and striations (grooves or scratches arranged in parallel series) on mountainsides that he came to believe were evidence of the passage of immense rivers of ice, called glaciers. He concluded that the formation of the Sierra canyons and ravines was the result of glaciers' relentlessly forcing their way through the surrounding mountains, pushing ridges of dirt and rock, called moraines, ahead of them.

Muir tried to correlate the great variety of rocks and sediments deposited in Yosemite's canyons and mountains with his studies of Louis Agassiz's theory of a great ice age. He came to believe that Yosemite Valley had been excavated by the constant movement of these glaciers over thousands of years. The gradual erosion of the mountains had formed basins, canyons, and dramatically shaped cliffs and boulders. He summarized his impressions in his earliest journal entries during one of his first forays into the Sierras:

Only a few hundred yards below our camp the ground is bare grey granite strewn with boulders. . . . The boulders, many of them very large, are not in piles or scattered like rubbish among loose crumbling debris as if weathered out of the solid as boulders of disintegration. . . .

They look lonely here, strangers in a strange land—huge blocks, angular mountain chips, the largest twenty or thirty feet in diameter, the chips that Nature has made in modelling her landscapes, fashioning the forms of her mountains and valleys. And with what tool were they quarried and carried? On the pavement we find its marks. The most resisting unweathered portion of the surface is scored and striated in a rigidly parallel way, indicating that the region has been overswept by a glacier from the northeastward, grinding down the general mass of the mountains, scoring and polishing, producing a strange, raw, wiped appearance, and dropping whatever boulders it chanced to be carrying at the time it was melted at the close of the Glacial Period. A fine discovery this.[44]

A Heated Controversy Arises

Muir's conclusions were in direct conflict with the theory of noted geologist Josiah Dwight Whitney, who asserted that a great earthquake had formed Yosemite's geography and geology. Whitney explained his theory in his book *The Yosemite Guide-Book:*

During the process of upheaval of the Sierra, or after, there was at the

Yosemite a subsidence of a limited area, marked by lines of "fault" or fissures. . . . In other and more simple language, the bottom of the Valley sank down to an unknown depth, owing to its support being withdrawn from underneath.[45]

Many people at that time agreed with Whitney. Fueling controversy, when California newspapers began publicizing Muir's theories on glacial movement, Whitney denounced Muir's conclusions and jeered Muir as "a mere sheepherder."[46] But despite the popularity of Whitney's earthquake theory, Muir was not without his own supporters.

In August of 1870 he accompanied a geological expedition headed by Professor Joseph Le Conte from the University of California. Le Conte had learned of Muir's observations and had organized and equipped a party of nine students to explore the mountain summits above Yosemite Valley. Muir led the party to an elevation called Eagle Peak, from which they could view the entire expanse of Yosemite and its hinterland, or inland region. From this height they were able to trace the proposed course of the glaciers they believed had carved out granite pathways through the mountains. Le Conte, greatly excited by his observations, recorded his thoughts that evening in his journal: "I strongly incline to the belief that a glacier once filled the Yosemite."[47]

Muir and Le Conte formed a friendship during their expedition that would continue for several years. As they explored the mountains further, Muir pointed out additional evidence supporting glaciation, such as gouge marks visible in the mountain walls of deep canyons.

After several days with the expedition, Muir returned to his mill in Yosemite Valley. Le Conte continued his journey northeast to Lake Tahoe to search for further evidence of glaciation in that region, con-

"The Lord Has Written in Capitals"

The influence of religion on Muir's philosophy of life is apparent in a letter Muir wrote from Yosemite to his brother David in 1870.

"I am sitting here in a little shanty made of sugar pine shingles this Sabbath evening. I have not been at church a single time since leaving home. Yet this glorious valley might well be called a church, for every lover of the great Creator who comes within the broad overwhelming influences of the place fails not to worship as he never did before. The glory of the Lord is upon all his works; it is written plainly upon all the fields of every clime, and upon every sky, but here in this place of surpassing glory the Lord has written in capitals, I hope that one day you will see and read with your own eyes."

vinced of the soundness of what he described as Muir's "discovery."[48]

Notwithstanding Le Conte's support of his theory, Muir felt driven to demonstrate conclusively the scientific validity of his discovery. Muir's desire to continue his research in the mountains conflicted, on the other hand, with a growing anxiety about his future and the necessity of earning a living. This ambivalence is reflected in a journal entry:

> There are eight members in our family [Muir excludes his mother here]. . . . All are useful members of society—save me. One is a healer of the sick. Another a merchant, and a deacon in good standing. The rest school teachers and farmers' wives—all exemplary, stable, anti-revolutionary. Surely then, thought I, one may be spared for so fine an experiment.[49]

An Unforgettable Visitor

In the midst of these anxieties about his future Muir was introduced to the famous American poet and philosopher Ralph Waldo Emerson. Emerson arrived in Yosemite Valley in the spring of 1871, and Muir was selected to serve as a guide during his visit to the Sierras. In many happy hours of conversation Emerson, thirty-five years Muir's elder, inspired Muir with his belief that all persons possessed the right to pursue their individual destiny in life.

The meeting proved to have a great influence upon Muir's life. Emerson's conviction encouraged Muir to continue his studies and explorations in the mountains. In later years, Muir remembered Emerson in his memoirs with quiet reverence:

Muir, who served as a guide when Ralph Waldo Emerson visited the Yosemite Valley in 1871, called the famous poet "a serene, majestic, sequoia-like soul."

Emerson was the most serene, majestic, sequoia-like soul I ever met. His smile was as sweet and calm as morning light on mountains. There was a wonderful charm in his presence; his smile, serene eye, his voice, his manner, were all sensed at once by everybody.

I felt here was the man I had been seeking. The Sierra, I was sure, wanted to see him, and he must not go before granting them an interview! He was as sincere as the trees, his eye sincere as the sun.[50]

Emerson, in turn, was very impressed by the tall, bearded man who had confided to him his intense love of the wilderness. At the end of his visit, as the

A Vigorous Existence

In a journal entry quoted in John of the Mountains *Muir enthusiastically describes his enjoyment of robust exercise combined with intimate encounters with nature.*

"Gain health from lusty, heroic exercise, from free, firm-nerved adventures without anxiety in them, with rhythmic leg motion in runs over boulders requiring quick decision for every step. Fording streams, tingling with flesh bruises as we slide down white slopes thatched with close snow-pressed chaparrall, half swimming or flying or slipping—all these make good counter irritants. Then enjoy the utter peace and solemnity of the trees and stars. Find many a plant and bird living sequestered in hollows and dells—little chambers in the hills. Feel a mysterious presence in a thousand coy hiding things."

philosopher made his way westward out of the Yosemite Valley, he turned to his companions and remarked, "There is a young man from whom we shall hear."[51]

Discovery of a Living Glacier

On July 10, 1871, Muir quit his job at the Hutchings sawmill. Carrying only a few belongings and a small provision of bread and tea, Muir made his way into the high country of the Sierras to continue exploring mountain summits and canyons. The manner of Muir's research during this time was carefully recorded in his journal:

This was my "method of study": I drifted about from rock to rock, from stream to stream, from grove to grove. Where night found me, there I camped. . . .

When I came to moraines, or ice-scratches upon the rocks, I traced them, learning what I could of the glacier that made them. I asked the boulders I met whence they came whither they were going. I followed to their fountains the various soils upon which the forests and meadows are planted; and when I discovered a mountain or rock of marked form and structure, I climbed about it, comparing it with its neighbors, marking its relations to the forces that had acted upon it, glaciers, streams, avalanches, etc., in seeking to account for its form, finish, position, and general characters.[52]

Muir believed that his glaciation theory would gain credibility if he could uncover the existence of an active ice river, or what he called a "living glacier," one whose movements could be measured and whose effects were immediately visible. On the morning of September 6, 1871, Muir noticed a small deposit of freshly ground gray silt in a streamed of an elevation called Black Mountain. Excited, he hurriedly climbed the steep slope of the moraine above and gained his first view of a living glacier.

Muir continued his search for evidence of glacial activity in the mountains for the next two years. His explorations led him along the tributaries of numerous rivers and compelled him to scale several mountain peaks in the southern Sierras. On October 21, 1873, Muir became the first man to reach the summit of Mount Whitney, at 14,494 feet the highest peak in the continental United States, by an eastern approach.

In the course of his explorations Muir found sixty-five small living glaciers. Then, in December 1873, he traveled to the Oakland, California, home of two friends, Mr. and Mrs. J. B. McChesney, for a ten-month stay during which he wrote a lengthy summary of his discoveries. His paper was published in 1874 as a series of seven articles for the *Overland Monthly* magazine under the title "Studies of the Sierras."

But despite the publication of Muir's thesis many geologists failed to acknowledge the historical significance of his data and remained skeptical of his assertions. It was not until 1938, nearly seventy years after the publication of "Studies of the Sierras," that a representative of the U.S. Geological Survey issued a public statement officially acknowledging the validity of Muir's theory:

In neither the Yosemite nor in any other valley of its type is there evidence of any dislocation of the earth's crust. . . . On the other hand, there is

As part of his ongoing studies, Muir sketched this picture of glacial movement in an attempt to explain the deep scratches in a Yosemite plateau's surface.

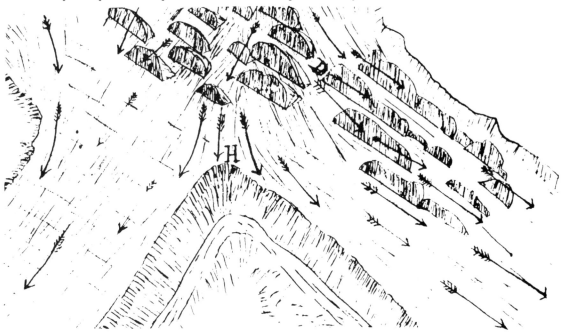

Thoughts of an Indian Summer

To Muir the change of seasons in the mountains was cause for spiritual celebration. In John of the Mountains *he reflects upon the peaceful beauty of summer's end.*

"Calm, thoughtful, peace and hushed rest—the pause before passing into winter. The birds gathering to go, and the animals, warned by the night frosts, relining their nests with dry grass and leaves and thistledown. . . .

The sun glowing red; the mountains silvery gray, purplish, one mass without detail, infinitely soft. . . .

In holiday array all go calmly down into the white winter rejoicing, plainly hopeful, faithful . . . everything taking what comes, and looking forward to the future, as if piously saying, 'Thy will be done in earth as in heaven!'"

abundant proof of powerful glacial action as Muir had recognized. . . .

To one thoroughly at home in the geologic problem of the Yosemite region it is now certain, upon reading Muir's letters and other writings, that he was more intimately familiar with the facts on the ground and more nearly right in their interpretation than any professional geologist of his time.[53]

While publication of his articles may not have lent substantial currency to Muir's scientific theories, it did provide him currency of a different sort, and he considered the possibility of earning a living by writing. Returning to the mountains, he resolved to record his nature studies as material for future books and articles. Thus began a literary career in which he would write some of the most widely read books on wilderness conservation.

5 Living in Two Worlds

Having completed his articles for *Overland Monthly* magazine, Muir was eager to return to the mountains. He disliked the confinement of city living and believed it was in fact unhealthy. His discontent was apparent in a journal entry written in the autumn of 1874:

> When I first came down to the city from my mountain home, I began to wither, and wish instinctively for the vital woods and high sky. Yet I lingered month after month, plodding at "duty" [writing magazine articles]. At length I chanced to see a lovely goldenrod in bloom in a weedy spot alongside one of the less frequented sidewalks there. Suddenly I was aware of the ending of summer and fled. Then, once away, I saw how shrunken and lean I was, and how glad I was I had gone.[54]

Muir left Oakland for the Sierras in September 1874. Although he was elated to be back in the mountains, Muir sensed that his initial period of exploration was coming to a close. Shortly after his arrival in Yosemite, Muir wrote a lengthy letter to Jeanne Carr, who had befriended him as a student at the University of Wisconsin. In this letter Muir confided that he had reached the limit of his earlier naturalist studies of Yosemite and that he was ready for new challenges in wilderness exploration: "No one of the rocks seems to call me now, nor any of the distant mountains. Surely this Merced and Tuolumne chapter of my life is done. . . . I feel that I am a stranger here."[55]

Despite these longings Muir's love for Yosemite continued to deepen, and the magnificent valley remained Muir's favorite sanctuary for meditation to the end of his life. In a second letter written to Jeanne Carr, Muir admitted that his return to the forests of Yosemite had renewed his devotion to nature: "I am hopelessly and forever a mountaineer. . . . Civilization and fever and all the morbidness that has been hooted at me have not dimmed my glacial eye, and I care to live only to entice people to look at Nature's loveliness. My own special self is nothing."[56]

New Mountain Explorations

Excited by the prospect of exploring new wilderness regions, Muir set out on October 15, 1874, for Mount Shasta, a volcanic cone in the Cascade Range of northern California, by way of Lake Tahoe, a distance

Muir considered the magnificent valley at Yosemite the perfect sanctuary for meditation, visiting the area frequently throughout his life.

of more than 250 miles. Before embarking on his journey, Muir had agreed to write a series of letters describing his travels to be published by the *San Francisco Bulletin* newspaper.

His arrival at Lake Tahoe was a disappointment; Muir was saddened to see large barren areas around the lakeshore where great numbers of pines and firs had been cut for timber. From Redding, California, Muir walked north along a route known as the old California-Oregon stage road to the foot of Mount Shasta. Despite the long journey on foot, Muir felt instantly refreshed by his first view of the snow-covered mountain and conveyed this exhilaration in one of his letters to the *Bulletin:* "All my blood turned to wine, and I have not been weary since!"[57]

Despite the warnings of seasoned mountaineers that Mount Shasta could not be climbed so late in the year, Muir confidently set out to scale the mountain. On November 2 Muir reached the summit and spent two hours absorbed in tracing the pathways of glaciers that flowed incrementally along the mountain slopes in rivers of ice. Too late to make a descent, Muir noticed the approach of a severe storm.

Confident of his ability to withstand the extremes of nature, Muir found shelter in the hollow of a large lava block and built a small campfire. He estimated his supply of food to be sufficient for three weeks on the mountain summit if necessary. Building a wall of pine chunks to protect him from the wind, Muir settled into his refuge and waited for the storm to pass.

The blizzard struck the mountain, blackening the sky. Safe within his shelter, Muir contentedly recorded his observations of this adventure. On the third day of the storm Muir wrote:

Wild wind and snow. Drifts changing the outlines of mountains—pulsing outlines. Three inches of snow on my blankets. Sifted into my hair. Glorious storm! A fine Clark crow visits me, sits on cones of P. flexilis, and pecks them open. . . . The cone sometimes breaks off; he follows, diving like a hawk, picks up and carries to a limb.[58]

The following day a rider on horseback appeared. He was in fact a friend of Muir, Jerome Fay, who knew Muir was on the mountain. Anxious for Muir's safety when the storm hit, Fay had set out from the hotel at the foot of the mountain to find him. Although grateful for Fay's concern, Muir was actually disappointed that his adventure had been interrupted. Reluctantly he left his lava shelter and returned with Fay down the mountain.

Vivid Communion with Nature

Muir left Shasta at the end of December to call on some friends at their home in Brownsville, California. The town, surrounded by forest, was located between the Yuba and Feather Rivers. One morning during his visit a great windstorm arose in the forest, leading Muir on an adventure dramatized in *The Mountains of California:*

Instead of camping out, as I usually do, I happened to be stopping at the house of a friend. But when the storm began to sound, I lost no time in pushing out into the woods to enjoy it. For on such occasions Nature has always something rare to show us, and the danger to life and limb is hardly greater than one would experience crouching depressingly beneath a roof. . . .

After cautiously casting about, I made choice of the tallest of a group of Douglas spruces that were growing close together like a tuft of grass, no one of

Eager to explore new wilderness regions, Muir walked more than 250 miles until he reached the foot of Mount Shasta, a breathtaking northern California peak.

A Symphony of Waterfalls

Muir loved the sounds of the wilderness as much as he did its visual beauty. In an undated journal entry included in John of the Mountains, *Muir recorded his impressions of the thundering waterfalls of the Sierra Nevada.*

"In the warm sunny season of May and June, when the snow is melting fast, the falls play their loudest music. Heavy tones like those of a great organ and muffled thunderclaps and gasping, drumming sounds occur at variable intervals and are readily heard, under favorable circumstances, a distance of four or five miles. The Upper Fall possesses far the richest as well as the most powerful voice of all the valley falls. Its tones vary from the sharp hiss and rustle of the wind among the glossy-leaved live oaks, and soft, sifted hush tones of the pines, to the loudest rush and roar of storm-winds and avalanches among the crags of the summit peaks."

Muir listens to the music of the Vernal Falls in Yosemite.

which seemed likely to fall unless all the rest fell upon it. Though comparatively young, they were about 100 ft. high, and their lithe, bushy tops were rocking and swirling in wild ecstasy. Being accustomed to climbing trees in making botanical studies, I experienced no difficulty in reaching the top of this one, and never before did I enjoy so noble an exhilaration of motion. The slender tops fairly flapped and swished in the passionate torrent, bending and swirling backward and forward, round and round, tracing describable combinations of vertical and horizontal curves, while I clung with muscles firm braced, like a bobo-link on a reed.[59]

From this treetop Muir had an excellent view of the surrounding country with its grainfields, valleys, and rolling hills. Muir remained high in the branches of the spruce tree throughout the afternoon, savoring the sounds and fragrance of the forest: "I kept my lofty perch for hours, frequently closing my eyes to enjoy the music by itself, or to feast quietly on the delicious fragrance that was streaming past."[60]

In April 1874 Muir returned to Mount Shasta with his friend Jerome Fay to continue his exploration of that region. Once again a sudden storm struck while the two men were high on the mountain. To keep from freezing they were forced to spend the night lying on their backs in the mud of a natural hot spring. The night proved to be a terrible ordeal. The men's backs were nearly scorched from the heat of the mud, while the front of their bodies was frozen by exposure to the storm's frigid winds. Muir urged his friend to stay awake

and avoid breathing the toxic gases emitted by the spring.

By the next morning the weather had calmed sufficiently for the two men to drag themselves from the steaming mud and make their way back to their timberline camp. There they found friends, anxiously waiting, who carried the exhausted men down the mountain on stretchers.

Inner Conflicts

Muir's feet had been badly frostbitten during his ordeal on Mount Shasta, and he decided to recover in San Francisco at the home of a friend, John Swett, to whom he had been introduced by Professor Ezra Carr. Muir's great affection for the Swett family made him realize how much he enjoyed and needed the company of friends. Despite his intense love of the wilderness Muir often felt isolated in the mountains and had occasionally recorded these feelings in his journal:

> To ask me whether I could endure to live without friends is absurd. It is easy enough to live out of material sight of friends, but to live without human love is impossible. Quench love, and what is left of a man's life but the unfolding of a few jointed bones and square inches of flesh? Who would call that life?[61]

Muir's passion for solitude and his studies of the wilderness often conflicted with his need for human companionship. This conflict compelled him to spend much of his life alternating between two worlds: the world of civilized society and the primitive world of nature. Of course, had Muir *wanted* company in the wilderness, it is

The Divine Presence

Muir believed in a spiritual unity in nature. Included in The Life and Letters of John Muir, *Vol. 1, is this correspondence to Muir's friend Catherine Merrill dated June 9, 1872.*

"You say that good men are 'nearer to the heart of God than are woods and fields, rocks and waters.' Such distinctions and measurements seem strange to me. Rocks and waters, etc., are works of God and so are men. We all flow from one fountain Soul. All are expressions of one Love. God does not appear, and flow out, only from narrow chinks and round bored wells here and there in favored races and places, but He flows in grand undivided currents, shoreless and boundless over creeds and forms and all kinds of civilizations and peoples and beasts, saturating all and fountainizing all."

An 1896 photograph captures the splendor of Glacier Point, Yosemite. Muir believed that God created humans and nature as an expression of one love.

Throughout his life Muir struggled with the conflict between his passion for solitude and his need of friends.

An Enlightening Encounter

Meanwhile Swett also had introduced Muir to a writer and lecturer named Henry George. George had been researching the phenomenon of land speculation and the effects of industrial monopolies in California. In his lectures and pamphlets George had attempted to alert the public to economic inequities in the state caused, for example, by railroad grants and exclusive land ownership by wealthy landlords. In some instances, George asserted, single landlords owned land tracts as large as 100,000 acres. Such ownership often included certain water sources in the High Sierra that were held as private property and manipulated or diverted as the landowner wished. As a result many small ranchers in the valleys and foothills were deprived of irrigation rights and even driven off their land for lack of water.

George's arguments were a call to action to Muir, who had seen for himself the barren acres of forests resulting from indiscriminate logging practices of certain landowners. He agreed with George that the practices of such land monopolists must be thwarted in order to conserve the nation's natural resources and wilderness. Accordingly, in the summer of 1875 Muir bade farewell to his friends in San Francisco, and set out on his final excursion that year to the Sierras. Unlike that of previous journeys, Muir's purpose in returning to the mountains was neither geological nor biological research. Incensed by the growing danger to his beloved wilderness, Muir was determined to personally investigate the severity of environmental destruction and to inform the public of the growing crisis.

doubtful that many people could have matched his stamina, tenacity, and willingness to forego creature comforts for the rough beauties of nature. This was a man who considered hiking through twenty or thirty miles of unmarked brush and steep ascents a pleasant day's excursion.

Muir hoped to resolve this conflict by sharing with people less familiar with untamed nature his belief that man could find a peaceful happiness by living in harmony with nature in its wildest state.

While he convalesced in San Francisco, Muir continued to write articles on his naturalist studies and explorations. Encouraged by Swett to submit his work to magazines in the East, Muir sent an article, "Living Glaciers," to *Harper's Magazine,* which accepted it immediately.

6 Decisive Years (1875–1880)

When John Muir returned to the Sierras in the summer of 1875 he began the passionate campaign to preserve the American wilderness that he would wage for the remainder of his life. In July Muir traveled down the Sierras to Mount Whitney and onward to Kings River and Yosemite. One afternoon while hiking through the woods Muir discovered nailed to a pine tree a notice that read:

> We the undersigned claim this valley for the purpose of raising stock, etc.
>
> Mr. Thomas
> Mr. Richard
> Mr. Harvey & Co.[62]

This notice symbolized to Muir the growing threat of land monopolists to the wilderness. He responded by writing an angry letter to the *San Francisco Bulletin* urging all nature lovers to

> visit the [Yosemite] valley at once, while it remains in primeval order. Some twenty-five years ago, the Tuolumne Yosemite was made into a hog pasture, and later into a sheep pasture. The Merced Yosemite has all its wild gardens trampled by cows and horses. . . . All the destructible beauty of this remote Yosemite is doomed to perish like that of its neighbor.[63]

Muir intended to investigate further the extent of private land seizure in the Sierras. Accompanied only by a mule named Brownie, he spent the next four months exploring the sequoia woods and the ranges of the Sierras, everywhere interviewing people he encountered, from mill workers and farmers to mountaineers like himself.

An Imperiled Wilderness

From those contacts Muir learned that much of the prime land and water sources in the high mountains had been taken over by wealthy land speculators, powerful mill companies, and public utility corporations. Many farmers who were subsequently unable to pay the high water rates imposed upon them had been forced to give up their land. Those farmers who remained had organized as members of an agricultural association called Grangers, intending to lobby for their rights as property owners.

Muir was deeply moved by the farmers' plight. His compassion for their hardship intensifed his anger over the growing destruction of the wilderness.

A Crusader Emerges

In November 1875 Muir returned to the Swett home in San Francisco to write a series of articles advocating wilderness preservation. The destruction he witnessed in the Sierras provoked his thoughtful evaluation of humanity's responsibility to safeguard its natural environment. Years later Muir recalled an experience from that winter that led him to a poignant realization of the need for natural beauty in people's lives:

> After I had lived many years in the mountains, I spent my first winter in San Francisco, writing up notes. I used to run out on short excursions to Mount Tamalpais, or the hills across the bay, for rest and exercise, and I always brought back a lot of flowers—as many as I could carry—and it was most touching to see the quick natural enthusiasm in the hearts of the ragged, neglected, defrauded, dirty little wretches of the Tar Flat [a slum area] of the city I used to pass through on my way home. As soon as they caught sight of my wild bouquet, they quit their pitiful attempts at amusement in the miserable dirty streets and ran after me begging a flower. "Please, Mister, give me a flower—give me a flower, Mister," in a humble begging tone as if expecting to be refused. And when I stopped and distributed the treasures . . . the dirty faces fairly glowed with enthusiasm while they gazed at them and fondled them reverently as if looking into the faces of angels from heaven. It was a hopeful sign, and made me say: "No matter into what depths of degradation humanity may sink, I will never despair while the lowest love the pure and the beautiful and know it when they see it."[64]

Muir had became a public figure with the dissemination of his articles on glaciation and nature studies in the *Overland Monthly* and *Harper's Magazine*. Shortly after his return to San Francisco, he was invited by the Literary Institute of Sacramento to lecture at the Congregational Church there. Although shy and generally ill at ease at public gatherings, he reluctantly agreed to appear on the advice of an artist friend, William Keith. Hoping to bolster Muir's self-confidence, Keith offered to

The destruction of wilderness in the Sierras prompted Muir to crusade for its protection. His persistent efforts helped spark a nationwide conservation movement.

loan him a beautiful Sierra mountain scene that Keith had painted. Muir gratefully accepted the favor, along with Keith's advice: "Look at the picture, and you will forget your bashfulness."[65]

Keith's intuition proved sound. As he stood before his audience, Muir gazed at the beautiful snow scene on the painting and all of his fear left him. A newspaper account of Muir's lecture that evening enthusiastically praised his appearance:

He forgot himself and his audience, only remembering that he was to make clear some wondrous mysteries. . . . His manner was so easy and so social, his style so severely plain and so homely . . . as often to provoke a

With the encouragement of his friend William Keith, Muir overcame his shyness and began lecturing on wilderness preservation.

smile, while the judgement gave hearty approval to the points. Indeed, Mr. Muir was at once the most unartistic and refreshing, the most unconventional and positive adventurer we have yet had in Sacramento.[66]

Muir's initial success as a lecturer led to a speaking tour of several cities in northern California. Despite growing popularity as a speaker, however, Muir never completely overcame his uneasiness at public appearances. A close friend, Charlotte Kellogg, who was aware of Muir's extreme shyness, once commented, "He preferred a wilderness of wild beasts to a formal audience."[67]

A Plea for Government Action

Muir's belief in the necessity of government control of forests first appeared in an article published by the Sacramento *Record-Union* on February 5, 1876, under a caption that read:

GOD'S FIRST TEMPLES

How Shall We Preserve Our Forests?

The Question Considered by John Muir, the California Geologist—the views of a Practical Man and a Scientific Observer—a Profoundly Interesting Article.[68]

In this essay Muir urged public support of government action to save the forests and stressed the harmful economic effects of forest destruction from droughts and floods caused by land erosion. Although the article captured the attention of several legislators in Sacramento, it failed to

Literary Endeavors

Muir's work in nature studies and wilderness preservation are an invaluable part of his legacy of conservation. In a letter written to his sister Sarah Muir Galloway in 1877 and included in The Life and Letters of John Muir, *Vol. 2, Muir predicts the success of his early works.*

"You inquire about [my] books. The others I spoke of are a book of excursions, another on Yosemite and the adjacent mountains, and another 'Studies in the Sierra' (scientific). The present volume will be descriptive of the Sierra animals, birds, forests, falls, glaciers, etc., which, if I live, you will see next fall or winter. I have not written enough to compose with much facility, and as I am also very careful and have but a limited vocabulary, I make slow progress. Still, although I never meant to write the results of my explorations, now I have begun I rather enjoy it and the public do me the credit of reading all I write, and paying me for it, which is some satisfaction, and I will not probably fail in my first effort on the book, inasmuch as I always make out to accomplish in some way what I undertake."

stimulate any decisive government reform. Undeterred, Muir resolved to continue both his studies as a naturalist and his crusade for forest conservation.

An Adventurous River Journey

In May 1877 Muir traveled to Utah to trace the ancient glacial rivers of the Wasatch Range. On a side trip Muir went swimming in the Great Salt Lake; he described the experience in his journal: "It was the finest water baptism I ever experienced. . . . Salted, braced, I ran bounding along the beach with blood tingling as if I had discovered a new glacier."[69]

Upon his return from Utah Muir was engaged to lead a small party, including the English botanist Sir Joseph Hooker, on a field trip to Mount Shasta. The party boarded a steamboat and traveled up the Sacramento River to the home of Gen. John Bidwell, a widely respected statesman and horticulturalist, who was renowned for being one of the coleaders of the first organized party to reach California by crossing the Sierra Nevada. Bidwell and his wife decided to join the expedition.

The expedition was scientifically productive and, impressed by Muir, the Bidwells invited him to be their guest on their return to their home, Rancho Chico. While standing with General Bidwell on the landing of the Sacramento River one afternoon, Muir expressed his desire to

Knowing how strongly Muir felt about the study of the wilderness, Louie Wanda Strentzel whole-heartedly supported her husband's explorations, which often kept him far from home for long periods.

sail down the river and explore its banks. General Bidwell obliged his guest, instructing the ranch carpenter to build Muir a skiff in which to make the journey.

Muir christened the boat *Spoonbill.* He thanked his hosts, said goodbye, and rowed his little craft into the current of the Sacramento River with an American flag waving in the brisk breeze. Unfortunately the journey proved to be a perilous voyage. Muir was compelled to pilot his skiff through so many snags and hidden sandbars in the river that he decided to rechristen the boat *Snagjumper.*

Success in Love and Work

His river voyage ended, Muir returned to San Francisco and the Swett home in the autumn of 1877 to resume his writing. There he renewed an acquaintance with a young woman, Louise Wanda Strentzel, nicknamed Louie, and her family. Louie was the daughter of Dr. John Strentzel, a prominent rancher who had grown wealthy as a large landowner and fruit-grower in California. The relationship between Muir and Louie soon developed into a courtship and by the spring of 1878 the couple was secretly engaged.

In that same year Muir published his first article for *Scribner's Monthly* magazine, "The Humming Bird of the California Waterfalls." This article was extremely well received by readers and Muir became a regular contributor to the magazine. Robert Underwood Johnson, a *Scribner's* editor, nature lover, and poet, was deeply impressed by Muir's writing; their professional and personal association would continue for many years.

First Alaskan Adventure

In June 1878 Muir accepted an offer of one hundred dollars from the administrators of a nationwide Sunday school convention to deliver an address on glaciation before a large gathering in Yosemite. At the convention Muir was intrigued by an Alaskan missionary's descriptions of the massive glaciers in that region. The prospect of exploring the ice rivers of that wild frontier was irresistible to the adventurer in Muir, and he decided to make the trip. Louie agreed to postpone their wedding until his return.

On July 10, 1879, Muir sailed for Alaska from Portland, Oregon, aboard the mail ship *California.* As the vessel entered

Alaskan coastal waters Muir marveled at the serene beauty of the horizon. As he writes in *Travels in Alaska:*

> Rounding some bossy cape, the eye is called away into far-reaching vistas, bounded on either hand by headlands in charming array, one dipping gracefully beyond another and growing fainter and more ethereal in the distance. The tranquil channel stretching river-like between many, may be stirred here and there by the silvery plashing of upspringing salmon, or by flocks of white gulls floating like waterlilies among the sun spangles, while mellow, tempered sunshine is streaming over all, blending sky, land, and water in pale, misty blue.[70]

The *California* docked at Fort Wrangell, Alaska, on July 14, 1879. There he met a young resident missionary named S. Hall Young, who became Muir's friend and companion in exploration while in Alaska. Young developed a great admiration for Muir's vast scientific knowledge and deep love of nature.

One afternoon, when bad weather forced his chartered boat to idle in port, Muir announced his intention to scale a steep, jagged summit known as Glenora Peak. Young eagerly offered to accompany him and the two men began their ascent, with Muir in the lead, unaware of danger ahead. The climb proved extremely difficult. According to Muir's barometer they had climbed 950 feet when they came to a narrow shelf that twisted around a sheer

Lured by descriptions of massive glaciers, Muir voyaged to Fort Wrangell, Alaska, to explore the expansive wilderness.

cliff. Eager to view the sunset from the summit, Muir leapt over a gully about four feet wide, landed on the opposite side, and hiked on.

Suddenly Muir heard his companion scream. Hurriedly retracing his steps, Muir found Young sprawled face down on the brink of the gully, which plunged more than a thousand feet to a glacier below. Muir cautiously worked his way to a point where he could grasp Young's belt and the seat of his trousers and draw him over the brink. The helpless Young told Muir that he had fallen and dislocated both of his arms. Summoning all of his strength, Muir dug out a series of footholds and, maintaining a firm grasp on his companion, slowly lowered him down the thousand feet to the glacier and helped him back to the boat.

Muir spent the autumn of 1879 exploring the Alaskan coastline near Fort Wrangell and the inland regions of the Stickeen River. He made careful observations of glacial movements and their effect on the terrain, and recorded his studies in his journal. As always, there were astonishing incidents to relate as well. One Sunday morning, Muir left his companions in camp and set out alone in search of an inland bay of snow and ice that he had heard natives refer to as Sitadaka. Indians had told him that no white man had ever seen the bay and Muir could find no reference to it on his maps or charts.

The Spectacular Sight of Glacier Bay

Eventually Muir climbed to a high plateau and found himself gazing upon a spectacular sight. In his book *Travels in Alaska*, Muir recorded this account of how he became the first explorer to discover what was named Glacier Bay:

> I reached a height of fifteen hundred feet, on the ridge that bounds the second of the great glaciers. All the landscape was smothered in clouds and I began to fear that as far as wide views were concerned I had climbed in vain. But at length the clouds lifted a little, and beneath their grey fringes I saw

Love and Philosophy

Muir wrote this letter, included in The Life and Letters of John Muir, *Vol. 2, to Louie Strentzel, while sailing to Alaska.*

"My Own Dear Louie:
I'm now about as far from you as I will be this year—only this wee sail to the North and then to thee, my lassie. And I'm not away at all, you know, for only they who do not love may ever be apart. There is no true separation for those whose hearts and souls are together. So much for love and philosophy."

After climbing fifteen hundred feet to a high plateau, Muir gazed down upon the spectacular sight of Glacier Bay.

the berg-filled expanse of the bay, and the feet of the mountains that stand about it, and the imposing fronts of five huge glaciers, the nearest being immediately beneath me. This was my first general view of Glacier Bay, a solitude of ice and snow and newborn rocks, dim, dreary, mysterious. I held the ground I had so dearly won for an hour or two, sheltering myself from the blast as best I could, while with benumbed fingers I sketched what I could see of the landscape, and wrote a few lines in my notebook. Then, breasting the snow again, crossing the shifting avalanche slopes and torrents,

I reached camp about dark, wet and weary and glad.[71]

In October Muir, accompanied by Hall Young and a party of Indians led by a chieftain named Toyatte, set out in canoes and spent five days exploring the bay Muir had discovered and its fiords (narrow sea inlets). As they traveled through this coastal region, the party encountered numerous glaciers, including an enormous ice river later named Muir Glacier. Although Muir was eager to continue his research, harsh winter weather prevented further exploration. In November the party retreated to Fort Wrangell from Sitka.

Muir returned to the mainland in January 1880. Although eager for a reunion with Louie, Muir found it necessary first to satisfy several lecture commitments in Portland and San Francisco. Through these lectures, Muir hoped to earn enough money to meet the financial responsibilities of marriage.

"The Happiest Man in the World!"

In February Muir returned to the Strentzel home in the Alhambra Valley, and married Louise Strentzel on April 14, 1880. The marriage proved to be a turning point in Muir's life. Now forty-two years old, Muir had spent much of his adult life in solitude, exploring the wilderness and devoting himself to scientific study. As he matured, Muir came to realize that he did not want to spend his entire life alone.

While camped in the mountains, Muir had expressed his loneliness and the importance of love in occasional journal entries:

October, 1872: There perhaps are souls that never weary, that go always unhalting and glad, tuneful and songful as mountain water. Not so, weary, hungry me. In all God's mountain man-

During his Alaskan expedition, Muir explored a vast river of ice that would later be named Muir Glacier.

"The Great Round Day"

On his first trip to Alaska, Muir marveled at the perpetual daylight of the region. Included in John of the Mountains *is his journal entry describing this phenomenon.*

"I should like to sketch one of these Alaska summer days, however imperfect the sketch must be. It is a day without night, for it begins and ends at midnight, which is the low noon of the great round day. The sky is red and orange then, for clouds more or less distinct are almost always present. The day opens slowly, the center of greatest light insensibly increasing and circling round the horizon's rim; and when at length the sun appears, it is without much of that stirring, impressive pomp, that flashing awakening energy so suggestive of the Bible image of a strong man coming forward to run a race. The colored clouds with their dissolving edges seem to vanish as their color leaves them, sinking into a hazy dimness around the horizon."

sions, I find no human sympathy, and I hunger.[72]

March 12, 1873: "All human love is in like manner Divine Love."[73]

Friends who knew of Muir's many years of solitude were delighted by his marriage. Jeanne Carr expressed her happiness for Muir in a letter she wrote to Louie:

Before fame, and far stronger than my wish to see his genius acknowledged by his peers, I have desired for him the completeness which can only come in living for others—in perfected home relations.[74]

In another letter to her friend Mrs. A. G. Black, Carr wrote of Louie: "This is the only woman I ever knew who seemed a mate for John."[75] And Muir himself, in an elated letter to Gen. John Bidwell, confided joyfully, "I am now the happiest man in the world!"[76]

7 New Alaskan Adventures

With his marriage to Louie Strentzel, Muir assumed the typical responsibilities of a California landowner. As a wedding present to their daughter and son-in-law, Dr. and Mrs. John Strentzel had deeded Muir the original Strentzel ranch house and twenty acres of orchards and vineyards. The Strentzels had vacated the Alhambra house for a newly constructed sixteen-room mansion in nearby Martinez.

After their marriage in 1880, Muir and his wife Louie settled down on this California ranch. Though a successful rancher, Muir missed the wilderness and continued his nature studies during the slow growing seasons.

Muir was determined to prosper as a rancher. On the day after his wedding he began work in his orchards and vineyards, diligently planting and cultivating his land through the spring. The slow, less demanding season of ripening began in early summer and continued until harvesttime in October. Muir was encouraged by his wife to return each year to the wilderness during this slow period and continue his nature studies. For the next decade Muir would combine devotion to his family and domestic horticulture in the spring, autumn, and winter months with wilderness exploration and nature studies in the summers.

Although Louie was often concerned for Muir's safety during his explorations, she realized how vital his work was to him. Louie believed Muir would become a great conservationist. She touchingly expressed this in a letter she had written to him the year before their marriage:

Do not be vexed [upset] because I am not so eager and jubilant as your own strong spirit. You must know that my heart is in all your work and that I rejoice over your gains. . . . But . . . you are more precious to me than any work, and it hurts me to feel so utterly powerless in aiding you and shielding you from pain. . . .

Yet . . . I would not have you come away . . . though I long to see your face more than words can tell. . . . Oh, John, though my weak fears so often dim all else . . . sometimes I think I comprehend the delight and precious value of your work to your own soul. Knowing this, I dare not call to lead you from the way that you feel best, wherever it may guide.[77]

Return to Alaska

So it was that on July 31, 1880, Muir, with his friend Thomas Magee, returned to Alaska on the steamer *California* to resume his explorations. During the voyage Muir wrote his wife several letters vividly describing the journey and the ship's entry into the ice-choked coastal waters of Alaska. While en route Muir noticed a British warship harbored in the Canadian port of Victoria, British Columbia. To Muir, the vessel symbolized civilization's invasion of the last remaining regions of wilderness in the world. He wrote to Louie:

Her Majesty's ironclad *Triumph* is lying close alongside. How huge she seems and impertinently strong and defiant, with a background of honest green woods! Jagged-toothed wolves and wildcats harmonize smoothly enough, but engines for the destruction of human beings are only devilish, though they carry preachers and prayers and open up views of sad, scant tears.[78]

The *California* reached the Alaskan coastline on August 8. Muir's joy at returning to Alaska's primitive and beautiful wilderness is evident in *Travels in Alaska:*

How delightful it is, and how it makes one's pulses bound to get back into this reviving wilderness! How truly wild it is, and how joyously one's heart responds to the welcome it gives, its waters and mountains shining and glowing like enthusiastic human faces. Gliding along the shores of its network of channels, we may travel thousands of miles without seeing any mark of

Crevices cut through the top of Muir Glacier creating an interesting effect.
Muir returned to Alaska in 1880 to study and document glacial movement.

man, save at long intervals some little Indian village or the faint smoke of a campfire. Even these are confined to the shore. Back a few yards from the beach the forests are as trackless as the sky, while the mountains, wrapped in their snow and ice and clouds, seem never before to have been looked at.[79]

When they arrived at Fort Wrangell Muir and Magee were reunited with their friend S. Hall Young, who agreed to join Muir's latest expedition. Muir had decided to finance the entire venture himself; he planned to explore, by canoe, Sum Dum Bay and its tributaries, Taku Inlet, Glacier Bay, and Taylor Bay to study and document glacial movement and its geological effects on the mountains and rivers of the region.

New Discoveries

For company on the trip Young decided to bring along his pet dog Stickeen, named after a tribe of Alaskan Indians. Young was extremely proud of Stickeen; the high-spirited animal resembled a collie but was only about half a collie's average size. For all his love of wild creatures, however, Muir at first objected to allowing the dog along on the journey. He referred to it as "a helpless wisp of hair, a soft little lap-midget," and "an infernal nuisance."[80] Stickeen seemed unperturbed by Muir's apparent disapproval. On the first day, while the rest of the crew looked on in amusement, the little dog proceeded to board the canoe and curl up to sleep right beside Muir. From that moment Stickeen was considered a full-fledged member of the expedition.

After the reunion and a brief visit with his friends at Fort Wrangell, Magee returned home. Muir and his party departed Fort Wrangell on August 16, 1880, in a canoe about twenty-five feet long and five feet wide, equipped with two small square sails. Included in the party besides Muir and Young were three Stickeen Indian guides called Captain Tyreen, Hunter Joe, and Smart Billy.

That day the voyagers traveled up the mainland coast; by noon they approached Thunder Bay, named for the sound made by icebergs fracturing and falling before an inflowing glacier. Muir delighted in the great beauty of the region, as he writes in *Travels in Alaska:*

> As we floated happily on over the shining waters, the beautiful islands, in ever-changing pictures, were an unfailing source of enjoyment; but chiefly our attention was turned upon the mountains. Bold granite headlands with their feet in the channel, or some

broad-shouldered peak of surpassing grandeur, would fix the eye, or some one of the larger glaciers, with far-reaching tributaries clasping entire groups of peaks and its great crystal river pouring down through the forest between grey ridges and domes. In these grand picture lessons the day was spent, and we spread our blankets beneath Menzies [a variety of spruce tree] on moss two feet deep.[81]

Muir and his companions also marveled at the phosphorescent glow of the local waters, a strange and beautiful illumination produced by the absorption of radiation of varying wavelengths. After two days' travel the party entered the cold northern waters of a stream teeming with salmon. The silvery bodies of the fish flashed reflections of the phosphorescent light and the Indian guides exclaimed, "*Hi yu salmon! Hi yu muck-a-muck!*" ("Plenty of salmon. Lots of food!").[82]

Muir's party made camp at the head of the stream and feasted on the abundant salmon. Muir marveled at the great variety and bounty of fish. His notes recalling this

Tribute to Stickeen

Muir's affection for the little dog that accompanied him in Alaska was expressed in this journal entry as quoted in John of the Mountains.

"Stickeen's homely clay was instinct with celestial fire, had in it a little of everything that is in man; he was a horizontal man-child, his heart beating in accord with the universal heart of nature. He had his share of hopes, fears, joys, griefs, imagination, memory, soul as well as body—and surely a share of that immortality which cheers the best saint that ever walked on end."

Muir wrote fondly of his excursions to Alaska, calling the beautiful scenery "an unfailing source of enjoyment."

wilderness banquet prefigured the growth of Alaska's great fishing industry:

> Whatever may be said of other resources of the Territory, it is hardly possible to exaggerate the importance of fisheries. Not to mention cod, herring, halibut, etc., there are probably not less than a thousand salmon-streams in southeastern Alaska as large or larger than this one (about forty feet wide) crowded with salmon several times a year. The first run commenced that year in July, while the king salmon, one of the five species recognized by the Indians, was in the Chilcat River about the middle of the November before.[83]

Near Sum Dum Bay, the travelers found that the bay was filled with swiftly moving icebergs. Cautiously they threaded their way through the ice to clear waters and proceeded up the bay. Fourteen hours under way, Muir's canoe entered an eastern fiord named Endicott Arm. At the head of the inlet, Muir discovered a frozen cataract, or waterfall, cascading down from immense granite mountains. Suddenly, as Muir paused to make a sketch of the huge glacier, several icebergs broke loose from the massive walls and crashed into the river with a thunderous roar. The dramatic display deeply impressed Captain Tyreen. Turning to Muir, he announced in Chinook (through an interpreter): "The ice mountain thinks well of you. He is firing his big guns to welcome you."[84]

Once again under way, the party rounded a huge rock and discovered a second glacier. The next morning Muir, with Stickeen, set out to explore the high granite walls surrounding the glacier. Young stayed behind; although recovered from his ordeal on Glenora Peak, he had promised his wife that he would never again attempt climbs of more than a few hundred yards. Suddenly the glacier shot a massive iceberg two hundred feet into the air before crashing into the water below. From his vantage point on the cliffs, Muir guessed that the pressure propelling the ice upward originated from the glacier's base, nearly nine hundred feet underwater. The small party watched spellbound as the glacier repeated this activity several times during the two days that the travelers remained in the vicinity. Muir decided to name this dramatic and powerful ice river Young Glacier in honor of his missionary friend.

A Perilous Adventure for Man and Dog

On the evening of August 29, Muir's party approached the open waters of the Pacific Ocean and camped near the entrance to Taylor Bay. Muir had observed that all of the glaciers they had seen on the journey up to that time were shrinking. He concluded that Taylor Glacier was rapidly advancing. Huge shattered rocks and uprooted forest trees had been left in the glacier's wake. To Young, Muir announced

---

A Naturalist's Appraisal

Muir's appreciation of Alaska's scenic splendor and excitement over that region's primitive beauty were enthusiastically expressed in his book Travels in Alaska.

"To the lover of pure wildness Alaska is one of the most wonderful countries in the world. No excursions that I know of may be made into any other American wilderness where so marvellous an abundance of noble, new-born scenery is so charmingly brought to view as on the trip through the Alexander Archipelago to Fort Wrangell and Sitka. . . .

Day after day in the fine weather we enjoyed, we seemed to float in true fairyland, each succeeding view seemingly more and more beautiful of all. Never before this had I been embosomed in scenery so hopelessly beyond comparison."

his intention of exploring the glacier the following day.

Early the next morning, while his companions were still asleep, he set off alone and on foot to explore Taylor Glacier. However, despite Muir's protests and whispered commands to return to camp, Stickeen persisted in following him on his adventure. Together they made their way toward the left margin of the glacier through forests of fallen trees and up steep granite slopes. The terrain was so rugged that soon Stickeen's paws were bleeding. Muir fashioned moccasins for the dog's paws out of handkerchiefs and the little animal bravely continued the journey.

To cross the vast ice plain to the glacier's western shore, Muir and Stickeen had to leap across a maze of crevasses (deep openings) in the ice. Toward late afternoon many of the crevasses they encountered were far too wide to be leaped, however, and Muir was forced to hike up and down the glacier in search of ice bridges to cross.

Many of these bridges were extremely narrow, with knife-sharp edges. Muir found it necessary to smooth the surface with his hatchet and cut footholds so that Stickeen could follow. At 5 P.M., after exploring an immense cataract larger than Niagara Falls, Muir set out across the ice to return to camp. Low clouds obscured his vision and slowed his progress as he searched for a way back across the maze of crevasses.

At the edge of a huge ice canyon nearly forty feet wide, Muir realized that he and Stickeen were trapped on an island of ice. Searching along the length of the crevasse, Muir noticed a mere sliver of ice bridge spanning the canyon. Muir recalls their perilous escape from this glacial island in *Travels in Alaska:*

I decided to dare the dangers of the fearful sliver rather than to attempt to retrace my steps. Accordingly I dug a low groove in the rounded edge for my knees to rest in and, leaning over, began to cut a narrow foothold on the

---

Alaskan Jewels

In Travels in Alaska, *Muir gives a vivid account of the many varieties of Alaskan berries.*

"And the wet berries. Nature's precious jewelry, how beautiful they were!—huckleberries with pale bloom and a crystal drop on each; red and yellow salmonberries, with clusters of smaller drops; and the glittering, berry-like raindrops, adorning the interlacing arches of bent grasses and sedges around the edges of the pools, every drop a mirror with all the landscape in it. . . .

In the gardens and forests of this wonderful moraine one might spend a whole joyful life."

steep, smooth side. When I was doing this, Stickeen came up behind me, pushed his head over my shoulder and looked in my face, muttering and whining as if trying to say, "Surely you are not going down there." I said, "Yes Stickeen, this is the only way."...

I chipped down the upcurved end of the bridge until I had formed a small level platform about a foot wide, then, bending forward, got astride of the end of the sliver, steadied myself with my knees, then cut off the top of the sliver, hitching myself forward an inch or two at a time, leaving it about four inches wide for Stickeen.[85]

When he had reached the other end of the crevasse, Muir called to the little dog and attempted to coax it across the sliver of bridge. Muir had grown to love Stickeen and was determined not to leave him behind. His admiration for the dog's courage was expressed in a journal entry recalling Stickeen's escape:

But in his little hairy body there was a strong heart, for notwithstanding his piercing recognition of deadly danger, he was able to hush his screaming fears and make firm his trembling limbs.

At length, as with the hushed, breathless courage of despair, he slipped down into the shadow of death, the storm was not heard or seen by either of us. I saw only those pathetic feeble little feet as he slid them over the round bank into the first step. Soon the hind pair followed, and all four were bunched in it. Then he worked them down into the next notch, and the next, and hushed and silent, lifted

his feet slowly in exact measure; I breathlessly watching him walk along the narrow sliver, waited on my knees ready to help him up the cliff at the end; but when he reached it, he hooked his feet into the steps of the ice-ladder, and bounded past me in a rush.

How eloquent he became, though so generally taciturn [silent]—a perfect poet of misery, and triumphant joy! He rushed round and round in crazy whirls of joy, rolled over and over, bounded against my face, shrieked and yelled as if trying to say, "Saved, saved, saved!"[86]

At 10 P.M. Muir and Stickeen straggled into camp. Muir was given warm clothing, hot coffee, and a mulligan stew (the name given to stews made of whatever ingredients are at hand). When he had finished his meal and felt somewhat revived, Muir looked off in the direction of the exhausted Stickeen, who slept soundly. Looking up at his friends, Muir said, "Yon's a brave doggie."[87]

Final Adventures and Home

Muir was to share one final excursion with Stickeen on the last week of the expedition. Muir set out with Hall Young to explore Muir Glacier, discovered in Sitadaka on his previous trip. His paws again wrapped in handkerchiefs, Stickeen trotted alongside Muir and together they traveled nearly thirty miles across the glacier. On this excursion, Young and Muir planted stakes in the ice river to measure

Muir took extensive notes and drew numerous sketches of the striking landscape he encountered on his Alaskan travels. Pictured is Muir's sketch of the Muir Glacier.

its flow; they recorded its rate of advance as fifty to sixty feet every twenty-four hours.

In early autumn the expedition returned to Sitka and Muir bade farewell to his friends. Before boarding the steamer for the voyage home, Muir seated himself on a coil of rope and took Stickeen's head into his hands. Sadly he said goodbye to the little dog and promised to return one day for more adventures. Stickeen was carried to a canoe and rowed away. On the wharf Muir heard the dog's unhappy cries and watched the canoe sail downriver. Unfortunately, though Muir would return to the Arctic, he would never see Stickeen again.

Muir learned later that Stickeen was stolen by a trader, his fate unknown. But the little dog and their shared adventures on the 1880 Alaskan expedition remained vivid in Muir's memory. The spirited dog's valor and loyalty convinced Muir that all animals, as well as man, possess a soul. In his journal, Muir expressed this belief in fond recollection of Stickeen: "He was indeed a fellow-creature—a little boy in distress in guise of a dog."[88]

8 Caught Between Two Worlds (1881–1890)

Following his return from his second trip to Alaska, Muir spent the autumn and winter of 1880–1881 with his wife at home on their California ranch. In December Muir wrote his sister Mary with exciting news: "We expect a long visit from a relative of the family that will no doubt claim a good deal of my time. . . . That exacting relative has no name as yet. I mean a baby who is to appear in a month or two!"[89]

On March 25, 1881, John and Louie's daughter Annie Wanda was born. Muir

Muir at home on his California ranch. When his health began to fail, Louie encouraged him to return to the mountains to seek rest.

was more determined than ever to provide a prosperous life for his family. Despite his resolve, however, his health had begun to suffer under the workload of ranching, and he developed a bronchial cough and a severe case of chronic indigestion. Louie grew deeply concerned over her husband's condition. Although she repeatedly advised him to return to the mountains and seek rest he steadfastly refused to leave his family.

A Hazardous Enterprise

Also in late March, Muir accepted an invitation to attend a formal dinner in Oakland honoring Capt. C. L. Hooper and the crew of the vessel *Thomas Corwin*, who were about to sail for the Arctic in search of the steamer *Jeanette*, which had been reported missing over a year earlier. The *Jeanette*, commanded by Lt. George W. De Long, had vanished while exploring a remote region called Wrangell Land off the coast of Arctic Siberia. In the course of their rescue mission, the *Thomas Corwin* would also enter various unexplored regions of the Arctic.

At the banquet Muir, given the seat of honor beside Captain Hooper, declined repeated requests by the officer to accompany the expedition. He discussed the invitation with his family the next morning. Louie's father, John Strentzel, approved of Muir's refusal, and expressed his opinion that a married man with a child had no right to leave on such a hazardous adventure. Muir's wife said nothing during the breakfast discussion, but later, in private, she urged her husband to go on the voyage and assured him that she and their

daughter were both happy and well. Encouraged by his wife's confidence, Muir joined the crew of the *Thomas Corwin*.

Search for a Doomed Ship

The voyagers departed on their mission May 4, 1881, and through rough seas reached Dutch Harbor, on Unalaska, on May 17. In late May the ship crossed the Bering Sea to the Siberian coastline and headed north in search of the *Jeanette*. They stopped to trade for supplies and warm clothing at various native villages, where Captain Hooper learned that in September 1879 a whaler had sighted the *Jeanette* locked in ice fifty miles off the south coast of Herald Island.

He set a course for Herald Island, the ship plowing its way north through waters increasingly choked with ice. In late July Hooper moored the vessel to an ice floe one thousand feet off Herald Island and sent a landing party ashore in search of survivors from the *Jeanette*, but the island's sheer cliff walls forced the party to turn back.

Muir was put in charge of a second search party of three crew members. This time the men successfully managed to climb the snowcliff that spanned Herald Island. They climbed to its highest point, twelve hundred feet above the sea, and surveyed the island but could find nothing to indicate that the crew of the *Jeanette* had been there. Reluctantly they abandoned their search.

On August 12 the *Thomas Corwin* reached the coast of Wrangell Land. Hooper was reasonably confident that his men were the first to set foot in this iso-

On a stop from their search for the lost steamer Jeanette, *Muir and the rest of the relief expedition wait for supplies before reboarding the* Thomas Corwin.

lated territory and claimed Wrangell Land in the name of the United States. Hooper, Muir, and crewmen had been ashore, making scientific observations and collecting plants, for only a few hours when Hooper received a report that the ice lane through which the *Thomas Corwin* had reached the shore was rapidly filling with ice. Hooper was forced to recall his men and sail for the open sea to escape being trapped by the ice pack.

The expedition nearly completed, the *Thomas Corwin* dropped anchor at Point Barrow and prepared to return to the United States. Although they had been unable to discover what had become of the crew of the missing *Jeanette*, Muir was pleased with the scientific observations of the Arctic he made during the expedition. From Point Barrow Muir wrote Louie a letter briefly summarizing the expedition's achievements:

We will take no more risks. All is well with our staunch little ship. She is scarce at all injured by the pounding and grinding she has undergone, and sailing home seems nothing more than crossing San Francisco Bay. We have added a large territory [Wrangell Land] to the domain of the United States and amassed a grand lot of knowledge of one sort and another.[90]

In September 1881 the *Thomas Corwin* sailed for San Francisco. Muir did learn of the fate of the crew of the *Jeanette* after his return to California. In December Muir received the astonishing news that survivors had reached Russian outposts in Siberia. Incredibly, thirteen of the thirty-three seamen who abandoned their sinking ship on the edge of the Arctic circle survived the five-hundred-mile journey to safety.

Legislative Disappointments

Following Muir's return from Alaska in 1881, Sen. John F. Miller of California enlisted Muir's cooperation in drafting two bills to be introduced in Congress. The first bill proposed the enlargement of the Yosemite Valley and Mariposa Big Tree Grove, tracts of lands under public domain that Muir hoped would be set aside as national parks. The second bill proposed that a specially designated tract of land in California be set aside as a public park. To Muir's disappointment, both bills were defeated. The failure of these initiatives came as a bitter blow to Muir and he decided to return to the management of his own business affairs.

For the next six years Muir devoted his energies to the development of his ranch in Alhambra, California, and to raising his family. During this time Muir kept no journals and wrote nothing for publication re-

garding nature conservation. After many years of exploring, he had decided to enjoy the comforts of a sedentary lifestyle.

On January 23, 1886, Louie gave birth to their second daughter, named Helen. Muir continued to buy and lease land from his father-in-law and applied his scientific knowledge to developing high grades of fruit and to increasing productivity. As a result of his efforts, Muir became one of the most successful horticulturalists (experts in the science of growing fruits, vegetables, and other plants) in California. His success brought him the financial independence that freed him to pursue scientific study and political activism in the years to come.

After the births of his daughters, Annie Wanda (left) and Helen (right), Muir ceased his wilderness studies and devoted his energies to his family and the ranch.

Many years later Muir wrote a brief summary of his life during the decade of 1881–1891 in his memoirs:

About a year before starting on the Arctic expedition I was married to Louie Strentzel, and for ten years I was engaged in fruit-raising in the Alhambra Valley, near Martinez, clearing land, planting vineyards and orchards, and selling the fruit, until I had more money than I thought I would ever need for my family or for all expenses of travel and study, however far or however long continued. But this farm work never seriously interrupted my studies. Every spring when the snow on the mountains had melted, until the approach of winter, my explorations were pushed farther and farther. Only in the early autumn, when the table grapes were gathered, and in winter and early spring, when the vineyards and orchards were pruned and cultivated, was my personal supervision given to the work. After these ten years, I sold part of the farm and leased the balance, so as to devote the rest of my life, as carefree as possible, to travel and study.[91]

A Son's Sad Farewell

This period of prosperity and family happiness was not without sadness, however. Muir had not seen his father, Daniel, for many years. For much of this separation, Daniel Muir, increasingly frail with age, had been confined to his bed at the home of his youngest daughter in Kansas City. In 1885 Muir had what he believed was a pre-

After spending ten years at fruit farming, Muir dedicated the rest of his life to studying nature and traveling.

monition of his father's death. Despite the harsh treatment he had received from Daniel as a boy, Muir loved his father and decided to travel to his sister's home and visit him. In addition Muir persuaded both of his brothers and his sister Annie to accompany him and wrote letters to two other sisters, Mary and Sarah, urging them to join the family in Kansas City. Muir had been told by his brother-in-law that Margaret was too ill to make the journey. Years later, Muir described this family reunion at his father's bedside in his memoirs:

Thus seven of the eight in our family assembled around father for the first time in more than twenty years. Father

A Sad Eulogy

Despite the harsh treatment he had received as a boy, Muir was saddened by the death of his father. In a letter written to his wife October 6, 1885, and included in The Life and Letters of John Muir, *Vol. 2, Muir expressed sorrow and love for his father.*

"You will know ere this that the end has come and father is at rest. . . .

Few lives that I know were more restless and eventful than his—few more toilsome and full of enthusiastic endeavor onward towards light and truth and eternal love through the midst of the devils of terrestrial strife and darkness and faithless misunderstandings that well-nigh overpowered him at times and made bitter burdens for us all to bear. . . .

But his last years as he lay broken in body and silent were full of calm divine light, and he oftentimes spoke to Joanna [Muir's sister] of the cruel mistakes he had made in his relations toward his children, and spoke particularly of me, wondering how I had borne my burdens so well and patiently, and warned Joanna to be watchful to govern her children by love alone."

showed no sign of any particular illness, but simply was confined to his bed and spent his time reading the Bible. We had three or four precious days with him before the last farewell. He died just after we had had time to renew our acquaintance with him and make him a cheering, comforting visit. And after the last sad rites were over, we all scattered again to our widely separated homes.[92]

Despite Muir's devotion to his family, he remained dedicated to the cause of conservation. Louie sensed that Muir was torn between fulfilling his responsibilities as a husband and father and actively campaigning to defend the forests and wilderness from destruction. Muir had discussed with

her the prospect of writing accounts of his travels in Yosemite and Alaska and of his growing need to arouse public awareness to the cause of wilderness conservation.

A Healing Return to the Wilderness

Throughout their marriage Louie urged Muir to return to the wilderness whenever he needed to regain strength and spirit sapped by the labors of ranch work. The years he devoted to domestic duties prevented him from continuing his work in conservation and had damaged his health.

Although he had sold off portions of his ranch in the mid-1880s, Muir was still burdened by business concerns and the management of his remaining property. He lost weight and suffered from fatigue. In a letter to his brother David in 1887, Muir confessed his exhaustion: "I am all nerve-shaken and lean as a crow—loaded with care, work and worry."[93]

Ultimately, in July 1888, encouraged by Louie, Muir accompanied his artist friend William Keith on an excursion to Mount Rainier, Washington. Muir's health slowly improved during this trip and his spirits soared at returning to the wilderness. Despite persistent fatigue, he joined Keith in climbing to the summit of Mount Rainier in August. Of his ascent, Muir

With the hopes of improving his ailing health, Muir accepted the invitation of his friend William Keith (pictured) to make an excursion to Mount Rainier in Washington.

A painting of Muir's father, Daniel, by his sister Mary. Though Muir received harsh treatment from his father as a boy, he described his father's last years as "full of calm and divine light."

wrote rather sheepishly to Louie: "Did not mean to climb it, but got excited and was soon on the top."[94]

Muir realized on the trip how deeply he had missed the wilderness and how much he needed the solitude of the forests. One day, during a walk through the woods, Muir recorded his thoughts about the happiness and peace of mind he had rediscovered in nature:

> When one is alone at night in the depths of these woods, the stillness is at once awful and sublime. Every leaf seems to speak. One gets close to Nature, and the love of beauty grows as it cannot in the distractions of a camp. The sense of utter loneliness is

heightened by the invisibility of bird or beast that dwells here.

One feels submerged and ever seeks the free expanse. . . . In that zone below the ice and snow and above the darkling woods, where the sunshine sleeps on alpine gardens and the young rivers flow rejoicing from the glacial caves . . . perfect quietude is there, and freedom from every curable care.[95]

Louie Speaks Her Mind

Muir was not the only one to gain such insight. During her husband's absence Muir's wife had given deep thought to her husband's welfare and the importance of his work in conservation. She became convinced that the exertions of ranch work were a primary cause of her husband's exhaustion. While Muir was still exploring the slopes of Mount Rainier, Louie wrote a letter to her husband expressing her belief that he should devote the remainder of his life to his research, writing, and wilderness preservation activities:

> A ranch that needs and takes the sacrifice of a noble life, or work, ought to be flung away beyond all reach and power for harm. . . .

> The Alaska book and the Yosemite book, dear John, must be written, and you need to be your own self, well and strong, to make them worthy of you. There is nothing that has a right to be considered beside this except the welfare of our children.[96]

Muir returned to Seattle from Mount Rainier late in the summer to find Louie's letter awaiting him. By the time he returned to the ranch a few days later, Louie had already conceived a plan to lessen Muir's ranch responsibilities by gradually selling off large sections of their

A Modest Appraisal of Home Life

In a letter written to Muir's friend James Davie Butler in 1889, and published in The Life and Letters of John Muir, *Vol. 2, Muir gave a good-natured account of his life at that time.*

"You want my manner of life. Well, in short, I get up about six o'clock and attend to the farm work, go to bed about nine and read until midnight. When I have a literary task I leave home, shut myself up in a room in a San Francisco hotel, go out only for meals, and peg away awkwardly and laboriously until the wee sma' hours or thereabouts, working long and hard and accomplishing little. . . . During meals at home my little girls make me tell stories, many of them very long, continued from day to day for a month or two."

A journey to Mount Rainier renewed Muir's passion for the wilderness. Shortly after his trip, Muir reduced his workload on the ranch and resumed his nature studies.

remaining land. Heartened and freed by his wife's support, Muir felt renewed enthusiasm to resume his wilderness travels and nature studies.

An Important Reunion

Muir's literary career was given significant impetus the following year by his reunion with Robert Underwood Johnson. The two men had first met in 1878 while Underwood was employed as an editor for *Scribner's Monthly*. The magazine had since been renamed *Century* and Underwood

was now associate editor. Underwood arrived in San Francisco in early June 1889 to research articles on the California gold rush. Hoping to persuade Muir to resume writing for *Century* magazine, Underwood asked for Muir's help in recalling many early California pioneers with whom Muir had been acquainted.

The collaboration led Muir and Johnson on a visit to Yosemite Valley. During their camping trip in the Sierras, Johnson proposed that Muir initiate a campaign for the establishment of a national park at Yosemite. As part of this campaign Muir would write a series of articles for *Century* magazine to arouse public support,

"I Am Getting Literary"

In a letter to his wife in July 1889, included in The Life and Letters of John Muir, *Vol. 2, Muir reports proudly on the day's writing for* Century *magazine.*

"You must see, surely, that I am getting literary, for I have just finished writing for the day and it is half-past twelve. Last evening I went to bed at this time and got up at six and have written twenty pages to-day, and feel proud that now I begin to see the end of this article that has so long been a black growling cloud in my sky. Some of the twenty pages were pretty good, too, I think. I'll copy a little bit for you to judge. Of course, you say, 'go to bed.' Well, never mind a little writing more or less, for I'm literary now, and the fountains flow."

describing the beauty of Yosemite and outlining proposed boundaries for the park.

Muir agreed to the plan. In August and September of 1889, he published two articles, "The Treasures of Yosemite" and "Features of the Proposed Yosemite National Park." The campaign did indeed generate nationwide support. In response to the impressive public enthusiasm, Gen. William Vandever introduced a bill including Muir's proposed boundaries into Congress.

A Fourth Trip to Alaska

In the spring after his articles appeared in *Century* magazine, Muir decided to make a fourth trip to Alaska to regain his uncertain health, explore the upper reaches of Muir Glacier and its tributaries, and await the fate of the proposed national park bill before Congress. On June 14, 1890, Muir left San Francisco for Glacier Bay. As always, once there he was awed by the primi-

tive beauty of this vast region. Encamped on an immense glacier one night, Muir recorded a poetic tribute in his journal:

> Divine beauty and power and goodness shining forth in every feature of the great icy day. Nature is seen at work transforming the whole face of the landscape, working in tremendous action, yet in perfectly poised harmony, disarranging nothing, the gardens growing calm in the midst of it all, the little birds and marmots fed, the streams singing while the mighty glaciers grind the rocks.[97]

A Renewed Sense of Purpose

Muir returned from Alaska in late July 1890 to find that the park campaign had generated great controversy. Opponents of the project attempted to discredit Muir by spreading rumors and printing false

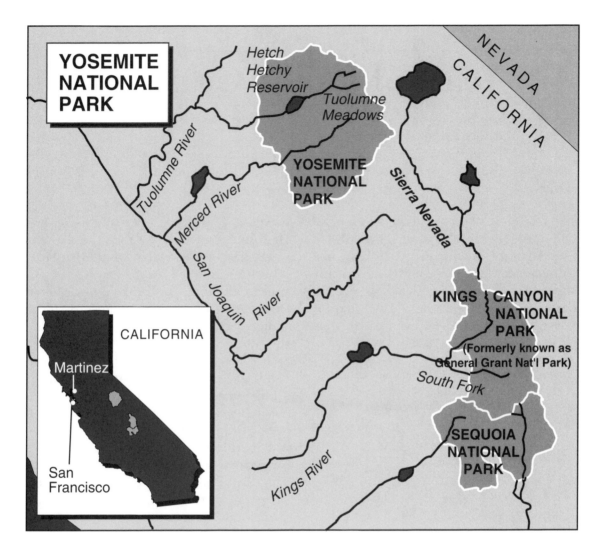

YOSEMITE NATIONAL PARK

Hetch Hetchy Reservoir

Tuolumne Meadows

Tuolumne River

Merced River

San Joaquin River

Sierra Nevada

NEVADA

CALIFORNIA

YOSEMITE NATIONAL PARK

KINGS CANYON NATIONAL PARK
(Formerly known as General Grant Nat'l Park)

South Fork

SEQUOIA NATIONAL PARK

Kings River

CALIFORNIA

Martinez

San Francisco

stories attacking his moral character, claiming that he was an unfaithful husband and an unscrupulous businessman. Despite such smear tactics, however, the project continued to gain political support. Secretary of the Interior John W. Noble, inspired by Muir's writings, had become convinced of the necessity of preserving the forested watersheds of America.

Realizing Muir's dreams of more than two decades, Congress passed the bill. President Benjamin Harrison signed it into law on October 1, 1890, and Yosemite was officially designated a national park. The bill also created the Sequoia and General Grant National Parks for the purpose of preserving other tracts of sequoia timber from further destruction.

The passage of the Yosemite National Park bill was a triumph for Muir and Johnson. This success inspired Muir to continue his campaign for increased government protection of the nation's timberlands and water resources.

9 Years of Public Crusade

The year of 1890 proved to be an eventful one in the life of John Muir. Through his collaboration with Robert Underwood Johnson, Muir had achieved significant success in enlisting political support for the cause of conservation. Muir's happiness over this progress was shadowed,

After the death of his father-in-law, Dr. John Strentzel (pictured), Muir administered the Strentzel family's large estate in addition to managing his own ranch. These responsibilities left Muir with little time to pursue his wilderness studies.

however, by the death of his father-in-law, Dr. John Strentzel, on October 31, 1890.

Following Strentzel's death, Muir moved his family into the Strentzel mansion in Martinez, California, in order to care for Louie's mother, and Muir assumed the responsibility of administering the Strentzel family's large estate. Along with the obligations of running his own ranch, these duties occupied much of Muir's time and energy for months.

Relief came in the form of his brother-in-law John Reid, who arrived in California in the spring of 1891 with Muir's eldest sister Maggie and their family. A long drought had forced Reid to sell his properties in Kansas and Nebraska and move west. Muir was overjoyed at their reunion. His sister had been frail since birth and suffered from ill health throughout her life. Happy to be given the opportunity to provide for her and her family, Muir offered the Reids a home on his ranch. In return, Reid agreed to assume many of the duties of ranch management.

Founding the Sierra Club

Throughout this deep involvement with family matters Muir had continued his

In 1890 Muir moved his family into the Strentzel mansion in Martinez, California, so they could care for Louie's mother.

Sierra Club. Included in the articles was a provision that clearly defined the Sierra Club's purpose:

> That the purposes for which this Corporation is formed are as follows, to wit: to explore, enjoy and render accessible the mountain regions of the Pacific Coast; to publish authentic information concerning them; and to enlist the support and cooperation of the people and the government in preserving the forests and other natural features of the Sierra Nevada Mountains.[99]

"Hilarious with Joy"

At the meeting John Muir was elected president of the new club. He was to hold that position until his death twenty-two years later. Muir was extremely proud of his association with the Sierra Club and believed that the organization would become a major force in forest conservation. Samuel Merrill, a close friend who was visiting Muir at his ranch when the Sierra Club was formed, later recalled Muir's joy at its creation:

friendship with Robert Underwood Johnson. Ever since their last reunion in 1889 Underwood had been urging Muir to "start an association for preserving California's monuments and natural wonders—or at least Yosemite."[98] Doubting his own leadership abilities, Muir had been hesitant to act upon this suggestion but the continuing destruction of California's wilderness through the greed and graft of private interests convinced him of the necessity of such an organization.

On May 28, 1892, Muir and a small group of friends met at the offices of prominent San Francisco attorney Warren Olney to draft the articles of incorporation for an alliance that they named the

> He came home jubilant from that meeting . . . and regaled them all with an account of it at the supper table. . . . I had never seen him so animated and happy before. . . . I venture to say it was the happiest day of his life. . . . Hitherto, his back to the wall, he had carried on his fight to save the wilderness. In the Sierra Club he saw the crystallization of the dreams and labor of a life-time. . . . He was hilarious with joy![100]

In a photo taken in 1909, seventeen years after Muir became president of the Sierra Club, Muir leads a Sierra Club outing. From its inception, the Sierra Club exerted strong political influence over conservation issues.

The political influence of the Sierra Club was tested shortly after its inception. In 1892 a bill was introduced into Congress proposing that a large tract of land including rich timber areas be cut away from Yosemite National Park, reducing the park to half its original size. The bill passed the House of Representatives by a large vote. Before it reached the Senate, however, Muir and the Sierra Club petitioned senators to defeat the bill. Muir dispatched numerous telegrams to influential government officials urging them to support the petition, and gave several newspaper interviews in the Eastern press to raise public awareness of the threat to Yosemite. The combined efforts succeeded; the bill was tabled by the Senate and eventually defeated.

Muir and the Sierra Club were further encouraged in their conservation efforts when president-elect Grover Cleveland assured Robert Underwood Johnson in 1893 that he would support wilderness preservation in office. In addition, prior to leaving office the departing Benjamin Harrison issued a presidential proclamation setting aside more than thirteen million acres of America's watershed land as forest reserves. Included among these reserves was the Sierra Forest Reserve in California, which covered more than four million acres.

Despite this official support, however, Congress had made no provisions to enforce the legislation by patrolling the designated forest reserves with federal officers. So the land was left unprotected, and stockmen and lumbermen continued, in defiance of law, to practice destructive grazing and timbering practices in these reserves.

East Coast Tour

In May 1893 Muir accepted an invitation from William Keith to accompany him on a tour of several cities on the east coast. The two friends met in New York and proceeded to travel north through Boston, Cambridge, and Concord, where Muir visited the graves of Ralph Waldo Emerson and Henry David Thoreau. Muir was very moved by his visit to the gravesites and expressed his feelings in a letter to his wife:

An early photo of a Sierra Club outing shows members using sticks to steady themselves on the icy mountain slopes.

Went through lovely, ferny, flowery woods and meadows to the hill cemetery and laid flowers on Thoreau's and Emerson's graves. I think it is the most beautiful graveyard I ever saw. . . .

Sweet kindly Mother Earth has taken them back to her bosom whence they came. I did not imagine I would be so moved at sight of the resting places of the grand men as I found I was, and I could not help thinking how glad I would be to feel sure that I would rest here.[101]

Back in New York, Keith and Muir attended a variety of social functions at which Muir was introduced to such prominent men of the day as Samuel Clemens (Mark Twain) and Rudyard Kipling. Muir was very surprised to discover that his writings and studies on wilderness conservation had made him a celebrity as well. In a letter home he modestly confessed: "I had no idea I was so well known, considering how little I have written."[102]

Return to Scotland

When they had concluded their tour in the East, the two friends parted ways, Keith to a tour of Europe, and Muir to his first visit to Scotland in more than forty years. On June 26, 1893, he sailed for Liverpool and made his way to Edinburgh. For the next two months he renewed his acquaintance with the country and its people.

At Edinburgh, Muir called upon the prominent Scottish book publisher David Douglas and the two men spent the night discussing literature and philosophy. Muir was extremely impressed by Douglas and wrote an enthusiastic account of their meeting to Louie:

In the evening I dined with him [Douglas] and had a glorious time. He showed me his literary treasures and curiosities, told endless anecdotes of John Brown, Walter Scott, Hugh Miller, etc., while I, of course, told my icy tales until very late—or early—the most wonderful night as far as human-

An Uplifting Counsel of Friendship

In this excerpt from a 1910 letter Muir counsels an old friend with some serene philosophical thoughts.

"Be of good cheer, make the best of whatever befalls; keep as near to headquarters as you may, and you will surely triumph over the ills of life, its frets and cares, with all other vermin of either earth or sky.

I'm ashamed to have enjoyed my visit [his life on earth] so much. A lone good soul can still work miracles, charm an outlandish, crooked, zigzag flat into a lofty inspiring Olympus."

In 1893 Muir started his literary career with The Mountains of California,
*a collection of articles about his travels in the Sierra Nevada. An 1896 photo
shows a hiker on the summit of Mount Gould in the Sierra Nevada.*

ity is concerned I ever had in the
world.[103]

Muir continued on to Dunbar, where
he had lived as a boy. He eagerly explored
the streets of the town and revisited the
family house he remembered from childhood. In a letter to his daughter Helen,
Muir wrote a nostalgic description of his
visit:

> Are you all right? I'm in Scotland now,
> where I used to live when I was a little
> boy, and I saw the places where I used
> to play and the house I used to live in.
> I remember it pretty well, and the
> school where the teacher used to whip
> me so much, though I tried to be good
> all the time and learn my lessons. The
> round tower on the hill in the picture
> [a sketch drawn by Muir] at the begin-
> ning of the letter is one of the places I
> used to play at on Saturdays when
> there was no school.[104]

Muir returned to New York in September and found a telegram from his wife
waiting, suggesting that he meet with the
new secretary of the interior, Hoke Smith,
in Washington to discuss national conservation matters. Muir spent several days
conferring with Smith and several other
advisers to President Cleveland. Though
no official statements were issued, all expressed their support for wilderness
preservation.

The First Wilderness Book

While in Scotland Muir had given deep
thought to writing books based upon his
travels and nature studies, as he and his
wife had long discussed. Back in California in late 1893 Muir finally began work
on his first book, a collection of articles he
had written over a period of several years

Muir made many lifelong friendships. In a 1913 letter, included in The Life and Letters of John Muir, *Vol. 2, Muir reminisced with Catherine Merrill, who had nursed him during his youthful accidental blindness.*

"It is now seven years since my beloved wife vanished in the land of the leal [loyal]. Both of my girls are happily married and have homes and children of their own. Wanda has three lively boys, Helen has two and is living at Dagget, California. . . .

As the shadows lengthen in life's afternoon, we cling all the more fondly to the friends of our youth. And it is with the warmest gratitude that I recall the kindness of all your family when I was lying in darkness. That Heaven may bless you, dear Mina, is the heart prayer of your affectionate friend."

regarding his travels in the Sierra Nevada. With the help of Robert Underwood Johnson, now his editor, Muir worked diligently to refine his writing into disciplined yet descriptive narrative.

The book was published by the Century Company in 1894 as *The Mountains of California*, and became an immediate popular and critical success. Charles S. Sargent, a Harvard botanist, wrote Muir an enthusiastic letter of praise:

> I am reading your Sierra book and I want to tell you that I have never read descriptions of trees that so picture them to the mind as yours do. No fellow who was at once a poet, naturalist, and keen observer has to my knowledge ever written about trees before, and I believe you are the man who ought to have written a *silva* [forest trees of a certain region] *of North America.* Your book is one of the great productions of its kind and I congratulate you on it.[105]

Encouraged by such praise, Muir pursued his literary career with renewed determination and enthusiasm. In addition to writing nature articles for *Century*, he began a new book focusing on his travels in Yosemite.

The Harriman Alaska Expedition

In May 1899 Muir accepted an invitation to join a scientific expedition to Alaska financed and led by a wealthy financier, Edward H. Harriman. The expedition would cruise the northern Alaskan coast, ostensibly gathering botanical specimens and studying the geology and glaciers of the region. Although Harriman and Muir became close friends during this journey, the expedition made very few scientific discoveries. Muir expressed his disappointment over what he perceived as failure (and suggested the real reason for the trip) in his journal:

> We had a long talk about book-making, with much twaddle about a grand scientific "monument" of the trip, etc. . . . Much ado about little. . . . Game hunting, the chief aim, has been unsuccessful. The rest of the story will be mere reconnaissance.[106]

In spite of his annoyance over the excursion's scant results, Muir managed to enjoy his fifth trip to Alaska and its spectacular scenery of immense glaciers and magnificent fiords. The voyage did provide him with some much-needed recreation, and he returned home to Martinez in mid-summer 1899 eager to resume his work with the Sierra Club and continue his writing.

An Eloquent Defender of Trees

In 1901 Muir's second book, *Our National Parks*, was published and again he attracted national attention. In this book Muir delivered an eloquent plea for forest preservation:

Muir, clutching a bouquet of wildflowers, and his friend John Burroughs on an Alaskan expedition in 1899.

Any fool can destroy trees. They cannot run away; and if they could, they would still be destroyed—chased and hunted down as long as fun or a dollar could be got out of their bark hides, branching horns, or magnificent bole backbones. Few that fell trees plant them; nor would planting avail much towards getting back anything like the noble primeval forest. . . .

It took more than three thousand years to make some of the trees in these Western woods—trees that are still standing in perfect strength and beauty, waving and singing in the mighty forests of the Sierra. Through all the wonderful, eventful centuries since Christ's time—and long before that—God has cared for these trees, saved them from drought, disease, avalanches and a thousand straining, levelling tempests and floods; but he cannot save them from fools—only Uncle Sam can do that.[107]

A Memorable Meeting

With the presidency of Theodore Roosevelt, the cause of wilderness conservation gained a powerful new ally in high office. Roosevelt assumed office in September 1901 following the assassination of William McKinley. The new president soon committed his administration to an intensive investigation of suspected corruption within the federal government regarding illegal land speculation across America. Assisted by Secretary of the Interior Ethan Allen Hitchcock, Roosevelt discovered a huge conspiracy of land frauds controlled by two San Francisco fi-

nanciers, John A. Benson and Frederick A. Hyde.

Together these men had illegally acquired vast tracts of land in California, Arizona, Utah, Nevada, Oregon, Minnesota, Nebraska, and Kansas. The investigation further revealed similar fraudulent land seizures in Washington, Oregon, Idaho, and Montana by other land speculators, involving senators, congressmen, judges, Land Office officials, and lumber, stock, coal, and copper syndicates.

Muir's crusade for forest preservation resulted in the federal protection of numerous forests throughout the United States. The Muir Woods (pictured) in the western Sierras are named and preserved in John Muir's honor.

The investigation triggered much controversy and vigorous opposition by numerous congressmen and syndicate lobbyists. Nevertheless, the courts, under Roosevelt's direction, issued indictments against accused conspirators that aided conservationists in protecting forest reserves from destructive land development.

Muir's work as a naturalist and conservationist had brought him national renown, and Roosevelt sought him out for discussions of national conservation issues. The president had received many second-hand reports by advisers regarding the destruction of national forests but Roosevelt felt that Muir could give him a more accurate assessment of the issues.

The president announced that he would visit Yosemite Valley in May 1903 and asked that John Muir join him as his guide. Muir agreed to postpone an extensive world tour to meet with Roosevelt. He realized that the president's visit to Yosemite would provide Muir with an excellent opportunity to lobby Roosevelt's continued aid in initiating government reforms in the cause of national conservation.

President Theodore Roosevelt stands with Muir on the rocks above the valleys and falls of Yosemite, California.

A Veteran Campaigner

In a letter written to Robert Underwood Johnson in 1905, Muir expresses a deep weariness.

"I am now an experienced lobbyist; my political education is complete. Have attended Legislature, made speeches, explained, exhorted, persuaded every mother's son of the legislators, newspaper reporters, and everybody else who would listen to me. And now that the fight is finished and my education as a politician and lobbyist is finished, I am almost finished myself."

In addition to conserving national forests, President Roosevelt declared numerous sites national monuments, including the Grand Canyon (pictured).

Muir and Roosevelt spent three days and nights together camping in the Sierra Nevada. During this time, Muir called on all his skills and experience to describe to the president the ruin of many timber and grassland areas in the country through destructive logging and grazing practices, and his belief in the critical need to initiate strong government policies that would protect the water reserves and forests of the nation. This first meeting between Roosevelt and Muir was the beginning of a friendship that endured to his death. Roosevelt was deeply impressed by Muir's passionate pleas and inspired by the grandeur of Yosemite. The impact of Muir's convictions upon Roosevelt was revealed in a public statement issued by the president shortly after his visit to the Sierra Nevada:

> No small part of the prosperity of California . . . depends upon the preservation of her water supply; and the water supply cannot be preserved unless the forests are preserved. . . .
>
> I ask for the preservation of other forests on grounds of wise and far-sighted economic policy. . . . We are not building this country of ours for a day. It is to last through the ages.[108]

During the remaining years of his presidency Roosevelt set aside 148 million acres of new national forests. In addition, Roosevelt was influential in passing the Monuments and Antiquities Act, through which Congress authorized the president to create national monuments by proclamation. Making the most of his increased presidential power, Roosevelt created twenty-three national monuments, including the Grand Canyon.

The Fight for Yosemite Valley

Shortly after his May 1903 meeting with Roosevelt, Muir began the recreational world tour he had postponed earlier. For the next year he traveled from Paris to Moscow to the forests of Russia and Finland, from the Himalayas to Egypt, Australia, Japan, and the Hawaiian Islands.

Muir returned home to find that the mismanagement of Yosemite Valley had become a national scandal. Although it had been designated as a national park in 1890, its administration was the responsibility of the State of California, which provided little oversight. Ineligible for protection by federal wardens, the park was at the mercy of loggers and sheepherders, who took advantage of the absence of government patrols to pursue illegal timber cutting and grazing on the land.

Muir and fellow conservationists, believing the situation was intolerable, initiated a passionate campaign for the recession (return) of Yosemite Valley to the direct control of the federal government. Debate over the issue of recession had been fierce since the creation of Yosemite National Park fourteen years earlier. With President Roosevelt's support, Muir requested that Sierra Club member and attorney William E. Colby draft a bill proposing the recession of Yosemite to the

federal government. In January 1905 the bill was presented to the California legislature, which passed the Recession Act on February 20. Despite this success, however, the battle was not won, as the Recession Act still lacked congressional approval. Opponents of the measure delayed its passage for over a year, attempting to alter the bill by proposing reductions of the park's boundaries.

Muir's political allies rallied to his support. President Roosevelt announced firmly that he would sign no bill containing boundary changes. On June 11, 1906, John Muir won his fight for the recession of Yosemite Valley and federal officials were dispatched for the protection of the national park.

Personal Loss

While the political battle raged, Muir had also been occupied with family concerns. His daughter Helen had suffered an attack of pneumonia, and her physician advised her to recuperate in the dry climate of Arizona. Muir had decided to accompany her. In late May 1905 they accepted an invitation to visit the ranch of Muir's friend Henry C. Hooker near Wilcox, Arizona.

On June 24, Muir received a telegram informing him that his wife had fallen ill and urging him to return home. Muir rushed to his wife's bedside to learn that a tumor had been discovered in her left lung. Doctors had no hope for recovery and on August 6, 1905, Louie Muir died of lung cancer. The death of his wife left Muir devastated with grief. For months he found it impossible to continue his writing, and instead devoted his time to the administration of his wife's estate. A close friend of Muir, C. Hart Merriam, sympathized with Muir's loss; he later recalled his impressions of Louie Muir and the role she and her daughters played in Muir's life: "She was a clever and noble woman, but so retiring that she was known only to a few. He [Muir] owed much to the sympathetic loyalty of his two daughters, Helen and Wanda, who, like their mother, were devoted to him and the work he was doing."[109]

Last Battle for the Wilderness

In 1907, fatigued and still grief stricken over his wife's death, Muir decided to accompany William Keith on a trip to a beautiful valley in the Sierra Nevada called Hetch Hetchy. Muir writes, recalling his friend's response to their surroundings:

The Muir family poses for a photo on the porch of their Martinez home (from left to right: Annie Wanda, Helen, Louie, and John).

Beautiful Hetch Hetchy Valley in the Sierra Nevada, pictured before it was flooded, became the site of Muir's last conservation battle.

The leaf colors were then ripe, and the great godlike rocks in repose seemed to glow with life. The artist . . . after making about forty sketches, declared with enthusiasm that although its walls were less sublime in height, in picturesque beauty and charm Hetch Hetchy surpassed even Yosemite.[110]

Hetch Hetchy Valley was to become the object of the final great conservation battle in John Muir's life. Muir's concern for the preservation of this valley originated in 1903 when the mayor of San Francisco, James D. Phelan, filed claims for the right to construct a dam, creating water reservoirs in a region of the Sierra Nevada that would necessarily involve flooding Hetch Hetchy Valley. The plan was vehemently opposed by Muir and the Sierra Club, which helped launch a campaign to block any legislation allowing such construction. The political battle between conservationists and supporters over the proposed dam continued for nearly a decade.

During this time, Muir devoted himself to raising public support and enlisting political aid for the preservation of Hetch Hetchy. Despite old age and failing health, Muir wrote letters, telegrams, speeches, pamphlets, and articles passionately denouncing the project. In his book

Though Muir fought to prevent the flooding of Hetch Hetchy Valley, his campaign failed. Muir was devastated when Congress passed a bill to construct the dam that destroyed the natural beauty of the valley.

The Yosemite, published in 1912, Muir included a stirring plea for the Hetch Hetchy's survival:

> These temple destroyers, devotees of ravaging commercialism, seem to have a perfect contempt for Nature, and, instead of lifting their eyes to the God of the mountains, lift them to the Almighty Dollar.

> Dam Hetch Hetchy! As well as dam for water-tanks the people's cathedrals and churches, for no holier temple has ever been consecrated by the heart of man.[111]

Despite considerable public support, Muir's efforts were futile. In the summer of 1913 Congress passed a bill granting the city of San Francisco rights to expand its water supply by flooding Hetch Hetchy Valley. To Muir's great sorrow construction of the dam commenced immediately, obliterating the natural beauty of what Muir described as "the sublime canyon way to the heart of the High Sierra."[112]

The defeat of the campaign to save Hetch Hetchy was a blow from which Muir never recovered. Muir's close friend Robert B. Marshall, of the U.S. Geological Survey, grieved to see its effect on Muir:

A Sublime Vision

In John of the Mountains *Muir reflected upon ageless marvels.*

"This grand show is eternal. It is always sunrise somewhere; the dew is never all dried at once; a shower is forever falling; vapor is ever rising. Eternal sunrise; eternal sunset, eternal dawn and gloaming, on sea and continents and islands, each in its turn, as the round earth rolls."

It was sorrowful indeed to see him sitting in his cobwebbed study in his lonely house . . . with the full force of his defeat upon him, after the struggle of a lifetime in the service of Hetch Hetchy. It was one of the most pathetic things I ever witnessed, and I could not but think if Congress, the President, and even the San Francisco contingent [supporters of the dam] could have seen him, they would certainly have been willing to have delayed any action until the old man had gone away—and I fear that is going to be very soon, as he appeared to me to be breaking very fast.[113]

"Death Is a Kind Nurse"

Old age did not diminish Muir's sense of wonder and belief in the harmony of nature. More than forty years had passed since Muir first embarked on his thousand-mile walk to Florida carrying his first journal, with its bold inscription, "John Muir, Earth-Planet, Universe." Near the end of his life, Muir looked back with a peaceful sense of completion, and ahead without fear:

Muir spends a reflective moment alone along a rocky trail.

The legacy of John Muir lives today in the splendor of America's national parks, which continue to serve as a tribute to Muir and his dedication to wilderness preservation.

All the merry dwellers of the trees and streams, and the myriad swarms of the air, called into life by the sunbeam of a summer morning, go home through death, wings folded perhaps in the last red rays of sunset of the day they were first tried. Trees towering in the sky, braving storms of centuries, flowers turning faces to the light for a single day or hour, having enjoyed their share of life's feast—all alike pass on and away under the law of death and love. Yet all are our brothers and they enjoy life as we do, share heaven's blessings with us, die and are buried in hallowed ground, come with us out of eternity and return into eternity. "Our little lives are rounded with a sleep."

Death is a kind nurse saying, "Come, children, to bed and get up in the morning"—a gracious Mother calling her children home.[114]

On Christmas Eve 1914 John Muir died peacefully in his sleep.

Throughout his life Muir remained an unassuming man who modestly described himself as merely a "mountaineer." His book and journals, which vividly described Muir's joyous solitary explorations of high mountains and deep canyons, captured the imagination of many nature lovers, who came to look upon Muir as a symbolic figure, a man truly living in harmony with nature. His public campaigns for greater government protection of America's wilderness regions helped spark a nationwide conservation movement. And the Sierra Club, which Muir cofounded, has become a major advocate for legislative protection of the American wilderness.

Muir was eulogized by many for his life's work in conservation. Perhaps one of the most appropriate assessments of Muir's impact upon the conservation movement was that of his longtime friend Robert Underwood Johnson, who in simple tribute said: "His work was not sectional but for the whole people, and he was the real father of the forest reservation system of America."[115]

Notes

Introduction: Devoted to Preserving the Purity of Nature

1. Linnie Marsh Wolfe, ed., *John of the Mountains: The Unpublished Journals of John Muir.* Boston: Houghton Mifflin, 1938.
2. Wolfe, *John of the Mountains.*
3. Wolfe, *John of the Mountains.*

Chapter 1: A Young Lover of Nature

4. John Muir, *The Story of My Boyhood and Youth.* Boston: Houghton Mifflin, 1913.
5. Muir, *The Story of My Boyhood and Youth.*
6. Muir, *The Story of My Boyhood and Youth.*
7. Muir, *The Story of My Boyhood and Youth.*
8. Muir, *The Story of My Boyhood and Youth.*
9. Muir, *The Story of My Boyhood and Youth.*
10. Muir, *The Story of My Boyhood and Youth.*
11. Muir, *The Story of My Boyhood and Youth.*
12. Muir, *The Story of My Boyhood and Youth.*
13. Muir, *The Story of My Boyhood and Youth.*
14. Muir, *The Story of My Boyhood and Youth.*
15. William Frederic Badè, ed., *The Life and Letters of John Muir.* Vol. 1. Boston: Houghton Mifflin, 1924.

Chapter 2: "John Muir, Earth-Planet, Universe"

16. Muir, *The Story of My Boyhood and Youth.*
17. Muir, *The Story of My Boyhood and Youth.*
18. Muir, *The Story of My Boyhood and Youth.*
19. John Muir, *The Yosemite.* New York: The Century Company, 1912.
20. John Muir, *A Thousand Mile Walk to the Gulf.* Boston: Houghton Mifflin, 1916.
21. Muir, *A Thousand Mile Walk to the Gulf.*
22. Muir, *A Thousand Mile Walk to the Gulf.*
23. Muir, *A Thousand Mile Walk to the Gulf.*
24. Muir, *A Thousand Mile Walk to the Gulf.*
25. Muir, *A Thousand Mile Walk to the Gulf.*
26. Muir, *The Yosemite.*
27. John Muir, *The Mountains of California.* New York: Century, 1894.

Chapter 3: "The Range of Light"

28. Muir, *The Yosemite.*
29. Muir, *The Yosemite.*
30. Muir, *A Thousand Mile Walk to the Gulf.*
31. Muir, *A Thousand Mile Walk to the Gulf.*
32. Muir, *The Yosemite.*
33. Muir, *The Yosemite.*
34. Wolfe, *John of the Mountains.*
35. John Muir, *My First Summer in the Sierra.* Boston: Houghton Mifflin, 1911.
36. Muir, *My First Summer in the Sierra.*
37. Muir, *My First Summer in the Sierra.*
38. Muir, *My First Summer in the Sierra.*
39. Muir, *My First Summer in the Sierra.*
40. Muir, *My First Summer in the Sierra.*

Chapter 4: Early Explorations (1869–1874)

41. Badè, *The Life and Letters of John Muir,* Vol. 1.
42. Wolfe, *John of the Mountains.*
43. Muir, *The Yosemite.*
44. Muir, *My First Summer in the Sierra.*
45. Quoted in Linnie Marsh Wolfe, *Son of the Wilderness: The Life of John Muir.* New York: Alfred A. Knopf, 1945.
46. Quoted in Wolfe, *Son of the Wilderness.*

47. Quoted in Wolfe, *Son of the Wilderness.*

48. Quoted in Wolfe, *Son of the Wilderness.*

49. Quoted in Wolfe, *Son of the Wilderness.*

50. Wolfe, *John of the Mountains.*

51. Quoted in Wolfe, *Son of the Wilderness.*

52. Wolfe, *John of the Mountains.*

53. Quoted in Wolfe, *Son of the Wilderness.*

Chapter 5: Living in Two Worlds

54. Wolfe, *John of the Mountains.*

55. William Frederic Badè, *The Life and Letters of John Muir.* Vol. 2. Boston: Houghton Mifflin, 1924.

56. Badè, *The Life and Letters of John Muir,* Vol. 2.

57. Quoted in Wolfe, *Son of the Wilderness.*

58. Quoted in Wolfe, *Son of the Wilderness.*

59. Muir, *The Mountains of California.*

60. Muir, *The Mountains of California.*

61. Wolfe, *John of the Mountains.*

Chapter 6: Decisive Years (1875–1880)

62. Quoted in Wolfe, *Son of the Wilderness.*

63. Quoted in Wolfe, *Son of the Wilderness.*

64. Wolfe, *John of the Mountains.*

65. Quoted in Wolfe, *Son of the Wilderness.*

66. Quoted in Wolfe, *Son of the Wilderness.*

67. Quoted in Wolfe, *Son of the Wilderness.*

68. Quoted in Wolfe, *Son of the Wilderness.*

69. Quoted in Wolfe, *Son of the Wilderness.*

70. John Muir, *Travels in Alaska.* Boston: Houghton Mifflin, 1915.

71. Muir, *Travels in Alaska.*

72. Wolfe, *John of the Mountains.*

73. Quoted in Wolfe, *Son of the Wilderness.*

74. Quoted in Wolfe, *Son of the Wilderness.*

75. Quoted in Wolfe, *Son of the Wilderness.*

76. Quoted in Wolfe, *Son of the Wilderness.*

Chapter 7: New Alaskan Adventures

77. Quoted in Wolfe, *Son of the Wilderness.*

78. Quoted in Wolfe, *Son of the Wilderness.*

79. Muir, *Travels in Alaska.*

80. Quoted in Wolfe, *Son of the Wilderness.*

81. Muir, *Travels in Alaska.*

82. Quoted in James Mitchell Clark, *The Life and Adventures of John Muir.* San Francisco: Sierra Club, 1980.

83. Muir, *Travels in Alaska.*

84. Quoted in Clark, *The Life and Adventures of John Muir.*

85. Muir, *Travels in Alaska.*

86. Wolfe, *John of the Mountains.*

87. Quoted in Wolfe, *Son of the Wilderness.*

88. Wolfe, *John of the Mountains.*

Chapter 8: Caught Between Two Worlds (1881–1890)

89. Quoted in Wolfe, *Son of the Wilderness.*

90. Badè, *The Life and Letters of John Muir,* Vol. 2.

91. Badè, *The Life and Letters of John Muir,* Vol. 2.

92. Badè, *The Life and Letters of John Muir,* Vol. 2.

93. Badè, *The Life and Letters of John Muir,* Vol. 2.

94. Badè, *The Life and Letters of John Muir,* Vol. 2.

95. Wolfe, *John of the Mountains.*

96. Quoted in Wolfe, *Son of the Wilderness.*

97. Wolfe, *John of the Mountains.*

Chapter 9: Years of Public Crusade

98. Quoted in Wolfe, *Son of the Wilderness.*

99. Quoted in Clark, *The Life and Adventures of John Muir.*

100. Quoted in Wolfe, *Son of the Wilderness.*

101. Badè, *The Life and Letters of John Muir,* Vol. 2.

102. Quoted in Wolfe, *Son of the Wilderness.*

103. Badè, *The Life and Letters of John Muir,* Vol. 2.

104. Badè, *The Life and Letters of John Muir,* Vol. 2.

105. Badè, *The Life and Letters of John Muir,* Vol. 2.

106. Quoted in Clark, *The Life and Adventures of John Muir.*

107. John Muir, *Our National Parks.* Boston: Houghton Mifflin, 1901.

108. Quoted in Wolfe, *Son of the Wilderness.*

109. Quoted in Wolfe, *Son of the Wilderness.*

110. Quoted in Wolfe, *Son of the Wilderness.*

111. Muir, *The Yosemite.*

112. Muir, *The Yosemite.*

113. Quoted in Wolfe, *Son of the Wilderness.*

114. Wolfe, *John of the Mountains.*

115. Quoted in Wolfe, *Son of the Wilderness.*

For Further Reading

William O. Douglas, *Muir of the Mountains.* Boston: Houghton Mifflin, 1961. Superior juvenile biography of Muir written with clarity and detail. The narrative includes many primary quotations.

Monte Dunham, *John Muir: Young Naturalist.* Milwaukee: Bobbs-Merrill, 1975. Juvenile biography stressing the childhood of the naturalist credited with incorporating Yosemite into the national park system.

Eden Force, *John Muir.* Englewood Cliffs, NJ: Silver Burdette Press, 1990. Straightforward juvenile biography of Muir recounting the conservationist's major contributions to wilderness preservation.

Roy Holway Jones, *John Muir and the Sierra Club: The Battle for Yosemite.* San Francisco: Sierra Club, 1965. Story of the Sierra Club's unsuccessful efforts to prevent Hetch Hetchy Valley from being dammed and flooded. Includes maps and illustrations.

John Muir, *Summering in the Sierra.* Madison: University of Wisconsin Press, 1984. Nature articles written by John Muir for the San Francisco *Daily Evening Bulletin* in the years 1874–1878.

Sally Tolan and G. Stevens, *John Muir: Naturalist, Writer and Guardian of the North American Wilderness.* Milwaukee: Childrens Books, 1990. A brief, simply written juvenile biography.

T. H. Watkins, *John Muir's America.* New York: Crown, 1976. Primarily pictorial volume chronicling John Muir's life and career. The book also contains numerous quotations from Muir's writings.

Works Consulted

William Frederic Badè, ed., *The Life and Letters of John Muir*. Vol. 1. Boston: Houghton Mifflin, 1924. Edited volume of selected journal entries and selected letters written by Muir during his youth.

William Frederic Badè, ed., *The Life and Letters of John Muir*. Vol. 2. Boston: Houghton Mifflin, 1924. Edited volume of selected journal entries and selected letters written by Muir during his later life.

James Mitchell Clark, *The Life and Adventures of John Muir*. San Francisco: Sierra Club, 1980. Excitingly written if somewhat uneven biography of John Muir emphasizing the adventurous career of the naturalist and his adventures in the American wilderness as well as in Alaska and abroad. Despite its interesting narrative, the book omits descriptive accounts of certain key events in Muir's career.

John Muir, *The Cruise of the Corwin*. Boston: Houghton Mifflin, 1917. Muir's account of his experiences with the crew of the vessel *Thomas Corwin* and their Arctic search for the crew of the lost ship *Jeanette*.

John Muir, *The Mountains of California*. New York: Century, 1894. Muir's first published book, a nature study, was extremely well received by the public. The book vividly describes the mountain and valley regions of the Sierra Nevada, including Yosemite National Park.

John Muir, *My First Summer in the Sierra*. Boston: Houghton Mifflin, 1911. Memoir recalling Muir's summer of 1869, spent in the Sierra Nevada range. Included are Muir's recollections of his experiences as a sheepherder and first impressions of the San Joaquin Valley.

John Muir, *Our National Parks*. Boston: Houghton Mifflin, 1901. Originally composed as a series of essays, the text offers an eloquent testimony by Muir for the need for national wilderness conservation. One of Muir's most ambitious and lengthy literary works, the book is in many sections highly scientific and technical in descriptions of plant and animal life.

John Muir, *Steep Trails*. Boston: Houghton Mifflin, 1918. A collection of essays that focuses primarily on the naturalist's recollections of scaling Mount Shasta and his travels through the mountain and valley regions of Nevada, Colorado, and Oregon.

John Muir, *The Story of My Boyhood and Youth*. Boston: Houghton Mifflin, 1913. John Muir's autobiographical account recalls events ranging from early childhood to his college years at the University of Wisconsin. Written with warmth and humor, the book offers valuable insights into Muir's character and personality.

John Muir, *A Thousand Mile Walk to the Gulf*. Boston: Houghton Mifflin, 1916. John Muir's memoir recounting his adventurous excursion on foot through the southeastern United States in 1867. Arranged partly in journal form, the book provides some interesting descriptions of post–Civil War America.

John Muir, *Travels in Alaska*. Boston: Houghton Mifflin, 1915. Muir's memoir recalling his scientific excursions in Alaska. At times thrilling, the book describes some hazardous treks undertaken by Muir in search of glaciers.

John Muir, *The Yosemite*. New York: The Century Company, 1912. Vividly written history and guidebook describing Yosemite Valley and its surrounding regions. As do many of Muir's works, the book includes many naturalist observations of plant and animal life.

Linnie Marsh Wolfe, ed., *John of the Mountains: The Unpublished Journals of John Muir*. Boston: Houghton Mifflin, 1938. Affectionately edited volume containing many journal entries composed throughout Muir's life. The book also contains the author's narrative introducing the periods of Muir's life chronicled in his journals.

Linnie Marsh Wolfe, *Son of the Wilderness: The Life of John Muir*. New York: Alfred A. Knopf, 1945. Entertaining and highly readable biography of Muir, chronicling the naturalist's life and career and offering thoughtful observations by the author on many of Muir's relationships with family members and friends.

Index

Picture Credits

Cover photo: Culver Pictures, Inc.

California Section, California State Library, 53

Courtesy of the University of Minnesota Library, 41

John Muir National Historical Site, 75, 83

John Muir Papers, Holt-Atherton Department of Special Collections, University of the Pacific Libraries. Copyright 1984 Muir-Hanna Trust, 9, 10, 11, 12, 19, 21, 37, 51, 54, 56, 60, 62, 64, 70, 71, 74, 77 (both), 82, 84, 89, 94, 98

Library of Congress, 91

© Michelle Morgan 1994, 90

Photo Researchers, Inc., 47

Sierra Club, 24, 26, 43, 50, 73, 85, 87

State Historical Society of Wisconsin, WHi (X3) 8575, 16; WHi (X3) 26656, 17; WHi (D487) 9783, 18

UPI/Bettmann, 57, 66

U.S. Department of the Interior, National Park Service, 33, 46, 79

U.S. Department of the Interior, National Park Service/Richard Frear, 31, 92

U.S. Department of the Interior, National Park Service/W. S. Keller, 59

Yosemite National Park Research Library, 34, 36, 38, 48, 95, 96

Yosemite National Park Research Library/Francis Fultz, 97

About the Author

Tom Ito is a freelance writer living in Los Angeles. His interest in the entertainment industry led him to publish *Yesteryears* magazine, a publication profiling television and radio celebrities, which he edited and distributed in the greater Los Angeles area from 1988 to 1990. Ito has served as a literary consultant to Hanna-Barbera Productions. He is listed in *Who's Who of Asian Americans* and is the author of a memoir, *Conversations with Michael Landon*.